ACCIDENTAL ACTIVIST

JOSH VENKATARAMAN
BARBARA VENKATARAMAN

Plan, What Plan?

I WROTE THIS BOOK TO SHOW YOU HOW TO GET STUFF DONE, important stuff that makes the world a better place. This is my primer for positive action and while I'm not sure how this happened, all of my advice starts with a "P". Sorry about that. I promise not to subject you to any more alliteration than absolutely necessary.

This book will take you through my quest for justice for The Groveland Four and teach you how to pursue your own endeavors, whatever they may be.

Before you jump in, what do you need to know? Well, here are a few things:

- Everything takes more time than you think.
- Nothing ever goes according to plan.
- Help can come from unexpected places.
- Time is on your side.
- Everyone is connected to everyone else (Six Degrees of Kevin Bacon).
- You can reach your tipping point for success and not even realize it.

- Your goals can change along the way.
- Flexibility is key.

If none of that resonates with you, don't worry, it will make sense later. Let's get started, shall we?

2

Famous People At A Party

I WAS BY FAR THE YOUNGEST PERSON AT THE PARTY AND THE one with the shortest bio. It was as if I'd wandered into a parallel universe, one where important people asked my opinion on things of gravity. I was Owen Wilson in *Midnight in Paris* when he meets F. Scott Fitzgerald and Hemingway--in a word, awestruck. But there I was, hobnobbing with famous authors as if I belonged.

I was a recent arrival to New York City, a college graduate starting his first job at a niche advertising agency. My life up to that point had been on a different plane entirely—happy hour after work with friends, same day theatre tickets, a pick-up basketball game, waiting for the F train, home decor from Target, and a slice of pizza from any establishment claiming to be Original Ray's, never eaten with a fork and knife because I didn't want to be laughed out of town.

Yet, on that particular day I was ten blocks from home and a world away, looking down at the glittering jewel-box of Manhattan from the forty-second floor of a beautiful apartment. I was petting a friendly dog named Louis and watching famous people play a game of Euchre while I soaked up the ambiance. I should have felt awkward but I didn't. I had brought a six-pack of Coney Island beer because I wanted to bring a good IPA but the host had it all covered with amazing barbecue and an excellent selection of wine and beer. At least I didn't come empty-handed.

Surrounded by Pulitzer-Prize winning authors and literary agents, I had no idea what to talk about. Our esteemed host, Gilbert King, had introduced me to the other guests like I was a VIP. Adam Johnson, author of *The Orphan Master's Son*, loomed as a larger-than-life figure and I watched him from a distance. Before I knew it, he and Gilbert had pulled me into the game and were trying to teach me how to play. I never quite caught on but I'll never forget how I felt that night, mingling with famous authors, on a first name basis with politicians and reporters, admiring the city from on high. And it all started with a book.

Passion Project

 *"Chase down your passion like it's the last bus of the night."*

Terri Guillemets

THE MOST IMPORTANT QUESTION TO ASK YOURSELF IS: WHY DO I want to take on this project? *Noblesse oblige?* A desire to help the less fortunate? Both are good reasons, but not good enough. A cause may be worth fighting for but if it's not causing you pain to think about it, if it's not burrowing under your skin to take up residence in your heart and mind, it's not for you. You can't look for a cause, it has to find you.

My project found me in early 2015, my junior year at the University of Florida. I was driving back to Gainesville from Orlando after a weekend trip when I saw a sign on the highway. It wasn't a sign from God but an actual sign with one word on it: "Groveland". Six months earlier that sign would have meant nothing to me but, in that moment, it opened my eyes to the past, to a tragedy that still echoed through the years. Seeing that sign made Groveland become a tangible place, a place where terrible things had happened. In 1949, where a white woman had falsely accused four young black men of rape and sparked a powder keg of racial upheaval, torture, murder, and hatred in a small town.

I'd recently read a book about it for my American History class: *Devil in the Grove: Thurgood Marshall, the Groveland Boys, and the Dawn of the New America.* The author, Gilbert King, had won a Pulitzer Prize for his work. I hadn't really thought about the book much besides the fact that it was a good read, it was just another assignment. Now I couldn't stop thinking about it. The fact that these guys were my age meant it could have been me. They were so young and they all had alibis, but it didn't matter. The fact that I had no idea this happened until I read the book and that it was so close to home, in places I recognized, made me realize this was real. It wasn't just a story anymore. Nothing was right about this case and I wanted--I needed--to do something to help.

As a twenty-one year old college student with no connections and no experience, I wondered what I could do about this injustice from more than sixty years ago. I was a telecommunications major with an interest in film-making so my first impulse was to create a documentary, but then I learned one had already been made. What did people do when they wanted change? They started a petition, of course. I'd signed a few petitions since turning eighteen but had never started one of my own. Honestly, I'd never done anything in the social justice arena before. Since fortune favors the bold I decided to contact the author, Gilbert King. To my surprise he responded to my email. He was kind and gracious and quite humble for someone with a Pulitzer Prize on the shelf. If it were me, I'd be working that beauty into every conversation. Take out the garbage? Sorry, no can do. I'm busy polishing my Pulitzer right now.

Gilbert appreciated my desire to help but told me a petition had been attempted before. I decided to go for it anyway. I couldn't give up before I started, right? Besides, if it were easy, the problem would have been solved a long time ago. I had to try. But there was someone I needed to find first, the woman who swore she would never stop until her father's name was cleared. I needed to find Carol Greenlee.

Posting A Petition

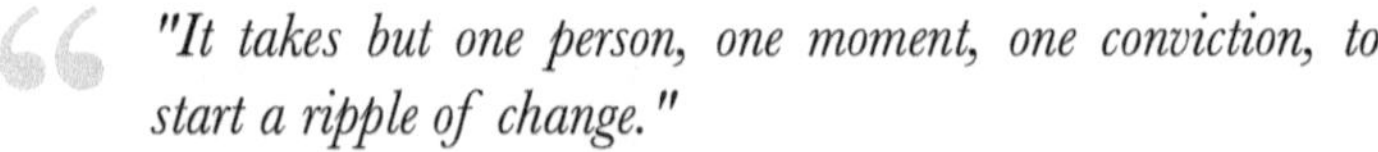

"It takes but one person, one moment, one conviction, to start a ripple of change."

Donna Brazile

IN THE OLD DAYS, A PERSON COULD WEAR OUT A CLOSET FULL of shoes collecting signatures on petitions. Now, thanks to change.org, you can share your petition with the world without ever leaving your chair. The downside is that you're competing with millions of other petitions all asking for just a minute of your time. Change.org is like a beauty pageant for the worthiest cause. It's hard to pick a winner when every contestant is praying for world peace.

Although it's free to post a petition, which is wonderful and egalitarian, if you want more eyeballs on it, you can pay for that. For a small fee, you can promote a petition (yours or someone else's) to ensure that it appears on other pages with similar causes. I learned this during my scouting expedition of their website. I was relieved at how user- friendly it was but intimidated by the sheer volume of competition. According to Wikipedia, change.org was posting five hundred new petitions a day in 2012. I could only imagine how many more were being posted in March of 2015 when I was getting started.

Before I could post anything I had a mystery to solve, a missing person case. She wasn't lost, she just didn't know I was looking for her. Carol Greenlee, aka Carol Crawley, was the driving force behind the exoneration effort. All four men had since passed on but their families were determined to clear their names, and nobody was more determined than Carol. Her father, Charles Greenlee, had been the youngest of the four and the only man not from Groveland. At age sixteen he had traveled to Groveland because his friend Ernest Thomas promised he would find work in the groves. Charles's fifteen-year-old girlfriend was pregnant and he wanted to provide for his baby (Carol), but he would never make it to the groves. While waiting for Ernest, Charles was arrested for loitering and hauled off. He would soon be accused of a heinous crime he couldn't possibly have committed, followed by beatings, torture, coerced confessions, a mockery of a trial, and a life sentence. He and Ernest would never meet again. When Ernest was also accused he fled town only to be shot dead as he slept under a tree, killed by a "posse" of a thousand Klansmen led by Sheriff Willis McCall, the "devil in the grove".

I learned about Carol through local news stories about the case. I also learned that other Groveland family members had sought the assistance of Geraldine Thompson, a state senator whose district included Groveland. At their request, Senator Thompson had submitted a bill to posthumously exonerate and apologize to the four men, specifically, to clear the names of Charles Greenlee, Walter Irvin, Samuel Shepherd and Ernest Thomas because of "egregious wrongs" perpetrated against them by the criminal justice system. The resolution also sought pardons for Irvin and Greenlee, the two men who survived to complete their prison sentences.

Senator Thompson explained why she thought this case was important: "The case of the Groveland Four is symbolic of the cases of many African Americans who did not receive fair treatment and equal justice in our Country. I feel that governmental officials should take responsibility for the actions of their agents and step forward to correct wrongs when they are identified. Many times an apology for wrongdoing on the part of governmental officials can help to bring about healing and reconciliation in the African American community. I believe action on this proposed legislation can help in efforts to ease racial tensions across America."

Despite her best efforts, which included buying forty copies of Gilbert's book and gifting them to her colleagues, Senator Thompson couldn't find a sponsor in the House and the bill died in committee. She vowed to try again.

That is how things stood when I decided to become involved. My mistake was assuming Carol still lived in Florida, which is why all my internet searches came up empty. I would have asked Gilbert for help but he had told me he wasn't in contact with any of the families. The only information I could glean was that Carol used the last name of Crawley as well as Greenlee. I turned to the best detective I knew, my mom. She was really good at finding people. It took her less than an hour.

"Did you look in Tennessee?" she teased me when she called.

"No," I said. "Why would I?"

"Because that's where her dad moved after he left Florida."

"But he's gone now," I replied.

"Well, she's still there!" my mom laughed. "And she owns a company too. Here's the phone number. Good luck!"

I practiced what I planned to say to Carol. I was nervous but not sure why. Fear of offending her? Fear of rejection? Fear of coming off as a crazy person? All of the above?

When she came on the line, I stammered through my speech, trying to explain who I was, why I wanted to help. She had a kind voice, although she did seem guarded. Who wouldn't be wary of strangers that tracked you down? For all I knew she had as many kooks calling her as I had telemarketers.

"You're a college student," she said, "Why aren't you just enjoying college life? Why do you want to help me?"

I told her I'd read Gilbert's book and she said she had too. How painful it must have been for her to read the grim details of what happened.

"I'd really like to help you," I said.

She paused. "Okay, why not? We need all the help we can get."

Months later Carol discussed that call in an interview. *It was a Sunday and I was sitting at my computer researching different agencies and organizations that assist innocent individuals incarcerated unjustly. I was at a dead end, frustrated, praying for a miracle, wondering if I would ever clear my father's name. I did not personally ask Senator Geraldine Thompson to sponsor the bill, but I followed it, and after it did not get through the process I felt defeated. When this college student called, I could not believe my ears. Something just clicked with Josh. I had already exhausted every avenue I had and then God sent me Josh out of the blue. I was floored.*

· · ·

I knew it wasn't God that had sent me to Carol, it was Gilbert. His powerful story shook me to my core. It was a story that still needed an ending.

———

Carol let me decide on the wording for the petition. She hoped it would help raise awareness of our cause. *Our cause*, I liked the sound of that. I knew that celebrities like Ashton Kutcher (and other less famous people) had started successful online petitions so I thought I could create a viral sensation and convince Governor Rick Scott to do the right thing. I had high hopes.

It was a complicated story to tell and my first attempt wasn't very good. Luckily, Change.org suggested ways to strengthen the message. I welcomed the advice--even if it did come from a bot parsing my words through an algorithm. Good customer service can take many forms.

Here is an excerpt of the Petition language: "The Groveland case was swept under the rug by all those involved and the state of Florida; many residents of Florida are not even aware this happened. The families of these men lost their sons, brothers, and fathers and we can't bring them back, but we can give them some peace of mind by having these men exonerated for a crime they clearly did not commit. Please help right this wrong by calling on Governor Rick Scott to exonerate the Groveland Four."

After posting the link all over social media I emailed it to my contacts. With two thousand Facebook friends I figured each one could sign the petition and then share it to double that number. Here's the part of the story where I obsess over the number of signers and refresh the link over and over but instead of HUGE SUCCESS flashing in neon lights in my brain, I see the words INCREDIBLE DISAPPOINTMENT followed by LAZY FRIENDS followed by NOT COOL! It reminded me of when I got my first email address at age nine. My dad set up my account and then I waited for the emails to start pouring in. When nothing happened I was upset. My parents gently explained that I had no mail because *nobody knew I had an email account.*

And here I was, waiting again. But this time was different; everyone knew about the petition and all they had to do was sign it. I had even promised my fraternity a keg of beer if a hundred of them signed. They ended up getting seventy-five so I bought them enough beer for a game of beer pong. I tried to stay positive whenever I spoke with Carol but she had to be frustrated too. She had paid to promote the petition on Change.org which had produced zero results. After three months of begging and pleading with friends in real life and on Facebook I only had two hundred signatures to show for it. If you subtracted my family and the families of the Groveland Four and my seventy-five fraternity brothers, it was downright pathetic. To put things in perspective, a current petition on Change.org is asking Ben & Jerry's for a new flavor called "Ruth Bader Ginger" and it has 8,500 signatures. Way more than two hundred.

I knew Carol was counting on me--and it wasn't just her. By then I was in contact with Charles's younger brother Wade, a pastor in Jacksonville, who had driven to Gainesville to meet me. I had also called Senator Thompson to tell her what we were doing and to offer my help, so I wasn't about to give up. I decided to reach out to the NAACP, the Innocence Project, and other social justice organizations, but none of them would get involved. I tried, and failed, to convince celebrities to Tweet about it. Some would raise my hopes only to dash them. I was starting to think the petition had been a colossal waste of time, a crapshoot that had come up snake eyes, but I couldn't have been more wrong.

Publicity, Please

"Publicity, publicity, publicity is the greatest moral factor and force in our public life. "

Joseph Pulitzer

AN AMERICAN NEWSPAPER EDITOR AND PUBLISHER, JOSEPH Pulitzer (1847-1911) was one of the most powerful and influential journalists in the country, a man dedicated to promoting social causes and exposing fraud and public corruption. It was his eponymous award, (one of the most prestigious in journalism) that had lifted Gilbert King's book into the spotlight and on to my reading list. For that I was grateful--but there was more. A second Pulitzer Prize winner (two in one story!) would boost our cause and change the history of the Groveland Four. His name was Leonard Pitts Jr.

———

With the petition floundering I searched my hometown newspapers for a columnist interested in criminal justice issues. I found Leonard Pitts Jr. at The Miami Herald and emailed him to plead our case in May of 2015. His quick response gave me hope.

"I was not aware of this story," he wrote. "Is there a book or newspaper/magazine story that documents this case? If so, it might be something that would make an interesting column."

I sent him a link to Gilbert's work and Mr. Pitts immediately replied that he had ordered the book and would take a look. "Maybe we'll talk later this year," he said.

That summer our petition had to fend for itself while I worked on building my resume. I had been selected for a highly competitive internship through the Television Academy Foundation and would spend half the summer in L.A. at USA Network. The other half would be spent interning for Washington Square Films in New York. The highlight of my stint at USA was when I was invited to pitch a script for a new series to network executives just for practice. It was both terrifying and exhilarating. In case you're wondering, my series was about a twenty-something guy who joins a traveling circus to prove to his ex-girlfriend that he's not boring. I knew about traveling circuses from working on a tent crew the summer before--but that's another story. Maybe USA Network will pick up my series one day and you can catch it there. Don't laugh, it could happen…

———

It was the end of August, the dog days of summer, when rich people leave town and college students return. I was looking forward to my senior year at UF where instead of making films for fun I would be graded on them--I couldn't wait to get started. I settled quickly into my old room in the apartment I shared with my buddies. I hadn't heard from Leonard Pitts Jr. all summer but not being shy I emailed him. He replied with four words that would change my life. He said: okay, let's do this. Progress at last! I told Carol the good news and we scheduled a conference call for the three of us to speak in September.

Hearing Carol's voice on that conference call was like reconnecting with an old friend. I had to remind myself I had only known her for six months and we had never met in person. It didn't matter, we were a team. Leonard Pitts Jr. was very interested in our story and asked pointed questions. I told him that when I saw the sign for Groveland on the highway I knew I wanted to get involved and change history, essentially.

When he asked Carol what motivated her to keep going she said this:

"You still have innocent people, innocent black men, every day being rejected, being dejected and being put in prison for things they have not done. So we've got to find a way to correct the injustice that a group of people have been experiencing for years. I'm 65 years old and I'm still looking for justice for my father who was wrongfully imprisoned for something he didn't do and really didn't happen. Why don't you correct that?"

In his column, Pitts would explain why our cause still mattered: "Some people like to pretend the world sprang into existence yesterday. In an era of mass incarceration and epidemic police misbehavior, they earnestly wonder why African Americans often don't trust law enforcement. Here, then, is an instructive reminder, past tapping present on the shoulder — justice denied for 66 years and counting."

Most importantly, he issued a call to action, posting a link to our petition with our plea for signatures. The column was published on September 26th, 2015 and it was excellent. I could say it was all we had hoped for but we had no idea what to hope for. We didn't have to wait long for results--people started signing our petition like crazy, people from all fifty states as well as other countries. That's when we realized Leonard Pitts Jr. was *nationally syndicated*! Who knew? Wikipedia did, but I must have missed that part when I read his entry. Even more rewarding than the signatures were the heartfelt comments people posted as their reason for signing. I was moved by the compassion and kindness, the support and outrage expressed. Carol loved the comments and called me to say she had stayed up all night reading them, smiling with tears of joy. Here are a few of them:

My heart breaks for these men and the families that live on after them. Although we cannot make them whole, we at least can, at last, let the truth be officially declared.

Justice, no matter how late.

Let justice be done. Or let the heavens fall.

Because right is right, because everyone should be ashamed that this was allowed to happen.

As a Floridian, I am also truly sorry and appalled.

NO one should be treated this way. They were never given a chance to prove their innocence.

I have a son and would hate for something like this to have happened to him. This had to be so painful for the families of these young men.

It's the right thing to do for these young men and their families.

I'm signing the petition, because as a criminal defense lawyer I believe the criminal justice system has become numb to the everyday injustices that occur in our courts. This is our chance to recognize one of those injustices, and hopefully help prevent similar incidents in the future.

I'm Florida-born and raised and only recently learned of this event, which leaves me deeply ashamed. We have a moral duty to deliver justice to the families of the Groveland Four.

I think it's a disgrace to humanity that such a thing happened and justice failed them.

I am deeply pained by what happened and upset that human beings can hurt others so casually. How can people have so much hate in them?

Two weeks later we had 3,680 signatures and I was able to convince the Daily Commercial, the Orlando Sentinel, and the Independent Florida Alligator (my school paper--their motto: we inform, you decide) to write about our project. Radio stations were contacting Carol for interviews and sometimes they interviewed both of us. I used our new momentum to ask for more publicity from local papers and TV stations. You know how it takes money to make money? It also takes publicity to get publicity.

Carol was overwhelmed by the reactions to Pitts's column and said it gave her confidence that her goals could be realized and the world would know the truth. She said the article had ignited a movement and fueled the fire and that even though there had been other articles, somehow the timing was right this time and a power greater than both of us was in the driver's seat.

As for me, I had an epiphany. I realized that, but for the petition, Leonard Pitts Jr. wouldn't have been as interested in our story. More than just the idea of exonerating the Groveland Four, the petition was an action item, something a UF student did as a step towards change. We weren't just wishing for a change, we were trying to make it happen and that made it easier to write about. Our petition was the key that opened all the doors.

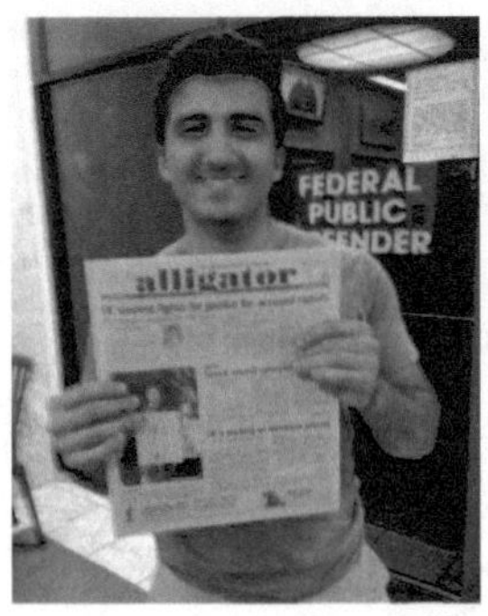

Gilbert's thoughts: Leonard Pitts is an excellent writer and someone I've been reading for years, so when his story appeared I was very pleased to see how much attention it received. Anything that increased attention was most welcomed, but to see that Leonard Pitts had written a story was a big deal. I knew how influential he is, and it was wonderful to see how the number of signatures began to grow.

Each interview with Carol gave me more insight into her backstory and into the man Charles Greenlee was. From the Independent Florida Alligator I learned that her father never missed her birthday when he was in jail and that one year he made her a jewelry box from matchsticks he found on the prison ground; how she didn't know why her father had been imprisoned until one New Year's Day in her early thirties when he finally told her. I learned how eloquent Carol is: "I will go to my grave trying to exonerate my father. An exoneration would ease the pain of a story never easy to tell. One day the scars will be healed."

From the Orlando Sentinel I learned how she had changed her name to Greenlee as a gift to her father on his sixty-fifth birthday and how he told her it was the best birthday he ever had. I also learned that besides fighting for justice she wanted the truth to come out to lift the cloud hanging over her family; that she couldn't understand why her father wasn't angry when he had been robbed of his innocence and his life and how he had explained "There are mistakes made every day. We have to find a way to forgive."

All this publicity brought more signatures and more Groveland family members into my circle. Vivian Shepherd, the niece of Samuel Shepherd, learned about the petition when the principal at East Ridge High School in Lake County where she worked handed her a copy of a news article. Walter Irvin's younger sister Henrietta, a woman in her eighties, contacted me through her grandson, who sent me a Facebook message.

When I returned to Fort Lauderdale for Thanksgiving the following month I was invited to visit Henrietta at her Miami home. By then we had over 6,000 signatures on our petition. Henrietta said she was thrilled with our progress. She was warm and welcoming and said her one desire was to live long enough to clear her brother's name. (She felt responsible for what happened to him but I wouldn't hear that story until the next time we met.)

Henrietta recounted what her family had gone through, how they had been en route to her brother Walter's execution when they heard on the radio that a last minute stay had been granted by the governor; how Sheriff Willis McCall had ruled Groveland by terror and wouldn't allow black people out of their homes if they weren't working in the groves; how he killed anyone who gave him trouble; and how there was so much blood spilled in the groves. I was surprised when she told me she knew Norma Padgett, the white woman who had falsely accused the Groveland Four of rape, and how Norma had been their neighbor back then and would bring them water when they were working in the fields; how Norma was still alive but had declined to comment or be interviewed in the six decades since passed.

Everything Henrietta told me that day in her matter-of-fact voice was chilling and surreal. This wasn't ancient history, these horrors had occurred during her lifetime. I left there even more determined to clear the names of these four men.

———

My dogged quest for publicity was paying off so I shouldn't have been surprised when Florida Trend Magazine decided to write a feature story about our petition--but I was, because it was me they wanted to interview. Carol was the one everyone usually asked. She was Gladys Knight and I was the Pips; she was Springsteen and I was the E Street Band---you get the picture. Of course, since she lived in Tennessee I was more accessible. Being unfamiliar with Florida Trend, I did some research and discovered a monthly magazine that covered Florida business, industry, education, and leisure with a readership of around 250,000. Their December issue was their most widely read as it listed the winners of their Golden Spoon Awards, the top dining spots in Florida. That was the issue I would be in. The opportunity to tell 250,000 more people about our petition was too good to pass up. Was I interesting enough to rate a feature story in an award-winning magazine? Only one way to find out, I said yes.

I didn't realize there would be a photo shoot and that it would happen in Groveland. At that point I'd probably said the word Groveland a thousand times but had never been there. Consider this: my hometown of Fort Lauderdale had a population of 180,000 while Gainesville, my then current residence, had 129,000 people, including 50,000 UF students. By contrast, just 11,450 people called Groveland home and, back in 1949, Groveland had only 1,024 residents. It was a small town with a big history and it was high time I saw it for myself.

A few days later, Ray Carson, the photographer, picked me up. During the ninety minute drive to Groveland I told him and his girlfriend its history, which they didn't know. Arriving in Groveland was like time traveling to bygone days. The main street with its little shops was exactly as I had expected, straight out of the 50's. There was some sort of election going on that day so, after we parked, we asked an older white woman with a campaign sign for directions to the courthouse. We said we were interested in landmarks pertaining to the Groveland Four.

"Oh, that," she said with a shrug, "That was all just a big misunderstanding."

I was flabbergasted. Torture and murder was a misunderstanding? Was this casual racism or total ignorance? Either way, I was glad Carol wasn't there to hear it.

We didn't go to the museum (which contained no reference to the Groveland Four, the torching of the black community's homes, the Klan, the National Guard, or Thurgood Marshall), but we did go to the courthouse, the same courthouse where Sheriff Willis McCall had beaten and tortured three young black men in the basement to coerce their confessions and later made them stand trial for a crime he knew they hadn't committed. Interestingly, the sheriff's office was located inside the courthouse and photos of every sheriff, along with their years of service, lined one wall of the corridor.

The infamous Willis McCall was there, having served seven consecutive terms, the longest of any sheriff. He would face no justice in his lifetime. I wondered if Alabama still proudly displayed pictures of former Governor George Wallace, known as "the most dangerous racist in America", in their public buildings. Like McCall, Wallace was the longest-serving governor in Alabama history, serving four terms. Unfortunately, the Deep South had a history of embracing the worst racists our country has known--and it was still happening.

Before reading Gilbert's book I didn't know that, in 1949, Florida was an epicenter of the KKK with Central Florida leading the way. There, elected officials, law enforcement, and prominent businessmen openly affiliated with the Klan. Driving through small towns on our way to Groveland and seeing Confederate flags on bumper stickers and license plates, often in the most impoverished neighborhoods, made me wonder: would the Civil War ever end?

I tried to answer that question in my Florida Trend interview. When asked why I believed it was important for The Groveland Four to be posthumously pardoned, I said this: "Having a huge injustice like this taints the name of Florida. I know there are hundreds of cases like this, but I guess this case sticks out to me as one that's horribly wrong in a state where a lot of horribly wrong things happen. Just fixing one of them, I think, would make a world of difference."

Public Participation

"One person plus one typewriter constitutes a movement."

Pauli Murray

IN DECEMBER 2015 MY WORLDS COLLIDED IN THE BEST WAY possible. I was invited to attend a multicultural career workshop in New York City and also invited to visit Gilbert King at his Manhattan apartment. The purpose of the workshop was to focus on my career (it's right there in the name), but I also used the opportunity to connect with a Huffpost Black Voices reporter who ended up helping with a Groveland piece for Reuters. It's all about the hustle.

When I met with Gilbert on my second day in the City we marveled at the success the petition was having and brainstormed about how to maintain the momentum. Yes, I was starstruck to finally meet the author who had inspired me, and yes, he was as excited about the project as I was. His book was having real-world consequences and making an impact and that has to be right up there with winning a Pulitzer Prize. Gilbert had an idea--why not go to UF and give a talk about the Groveland Four? I liked it but I knew our speaker program was already booked for the year, we had no money left.

Gilbert perked up. "I don't want to be paid," he grinned. "I just want to come speak."

"Oh, that changes everything," I said with a laugh.

We decided to approach both the Levin School of Law and the history department to see who was interested. Our plan was to invite Carol and Henrietta Irvin to join Gilbert on a panel afterward for a Q & A.

"And you," Gilbert said. "You have to be on the panel."

————

After both departments agreed to jointly host the talk it should have been smooth sailing from there, but it wasn't. I'm not saying I'm blameless, but just hear me out. You know the parable of the blind men and the elephant? One felt the tusk, another, the ear, a third, the leg, and a fourth, the tail, after which each thought he could describe the elephant.

It seemed UF and I had very different elephants in mind.

I saw the forum as an opportunity to include Black Lives Matter, the movement that started with a hashtag in 2013 when George Zimmerman was acquitted in the shooting death of seventeen-year-old Trayvon Martin in Florida (not far from Groveland). Since then, BLM had expanded to include issues of police killings of black people, racial profil-ing, police brutality, and racial inequality in the justice system, and had gone on to protest, among others, the deaths of Michael Brown in Ferguson, Missouri, and Eric Garner in New York City at the hands of police.

While Trayvon Martin wasn't killed by police like Ernest Thomas and Sam Shepherd had been, like them, Trayvon was a young black man whose death was enabled by a broken justice system, a system that provided a Stand Your Ground defense to a man who killed a child walking home from the store. Fifty miles and sixty-three years separated the deaths of Thomas and Shepherd from the death of Trayvon Martin but how much had really changed? Not much. Black lives didn't matter back in 1949 and they still didn't.

Unimpressed with my vision, the Levin School of Law saw the forum as an opportunity to host a Pulitzer Prize winner to discuss an historic legal case that featured a young Thurgood Marshall fighting for justice. While cognizant of the racial and social justice issues, they wanted to maintain decorum. In short, when I suggested a prominent black singer by the name of Charles Bradley perform at the reception (he had said yes, by the way!), they nixed it and stopped inviting me to the planning meetings.

In the end, it all worked out and I didn't miss the singer. Our forum was held on February 18, 2016 at the Levin School of Law with seventy people attending--including a surprise guest in the audience. As Gilbert prepared his PowerPoint at the front of the lecture hall I raced around outside directing various Groveland family members to the law school. I had a list of the people coming and wanted to make them all feel welcome. I was especially concerned about Henrietta Irvin who had agreed to speak on the panel. A frail eighty-two year old, she was traveling from Miami to Gainesville with her grandson.

Finally, I walked inside to find my parents who had driven up from Fort Lauderdale just for this event. They were deep in conversation with a woman they were excited to introduce.

"Josh," my dad said, "don't you know who this is? Say Hi to Carol Greenlee."

I turned to look at the smiling woman with close-cropped salt and pepper hair and, too emotional to say a word, we hugged each other like long-lost friends. For me, it was surreal, a moment frozen in time. I couldn't believe I was finally meeting her, the person I had up on a pedestal.

With no time to chat we took our seats next to Henrietta, facing the audience, as Gilbert, an excellent speaker, proceeded to explain the history of segregation, Florida's relationship with the KKK, Jim Crow laws, and the myth of separate but equal. He taught us the history we should have learned in school, providing the backdrop for the horrors experienced by the Groveland Four.

A panel discussion followed and Carol spoke about how bereft she felt growing up without her father, knowing he was in prison without knowing why, feeling the stigma of the crime he had been falsely convicted of. She didn't even use her father's surname because her mother didn't want her to be ostracized. She spoke about how her father harbored no anger but didn't believe in rehashing the past. He thought it would do no good for anyone.

Henrietta recounted how her brother Walter had served in the army during World War II and how after his discharge he had told his family he was not returning to Groveland. Henrietta wrote to her brother and insisted he come home to see his mother, and so he did. Two weeks later he was in jail for a crime he didn't commit. Henrietta was only sixteen at the time and had just married Sam Shepherd's brother.

"I didn't know what to do," she said, "because I was a kid. It just broke my heart. I knew he was innocent." It was clear that she felt responsible for what had happened to her brother. She said that even though he was gone she wanted to live long enough to clear his name.

When it was my turn, I spoke about my petition and how we had arrived at that moment, and then it was time for the Q & A. The audience was a mix of different age groups, different races, students as well as community members. There were reporters, of course, and not just the Independent Alligator-- although they were there too. Like the comments on our petition, many of the remarks from the audience were about their own experiences with racism, some suggestions for how to change things, and how much compassion they felt for Carol and Henrietta.

Then a young man stood up, his blond hair captured in a bun on top of his head. He introduced himself as Sam Harris and said that Sheriff Willis McCall, aka the devil in the grove, was his great-uncle. There was a ripple through the audience. He choked up and continued.

"I came here today," he said, tearful, "to apologize to the families of the Groveland Four." Then he sat down again.

There was a collective gasp and then the only sounds from the audience were sniffling and the rustle of Kleenex packages being passed around.

Carol broke the silence. "It's alright," she said. "I forgive Willis McCall, and you don't have to apologize for him."

Although I didn't have a chance to bring up the Black Lives Matter movement that day, it was on my mind when The Gainesville Sun asked me for a quote.

I said: "This case that happened 65-plus years ago is not that far off from cases that have happened a few weeks ago or a year ago. Sometimes you have to look back at the past to figure out what's going on in the future. If we can make this exoneration happen, I think that will ease some racial tensions and even lead to further exonerations. Looking at this case shows how little things have changed over the years."

RIP, Trayvon Martin.

———

Gilbert King: *I thought this event was important because it brought everything back to the University where Josh was inspired to take action. And now, the families were fully on board, and you could feel the momentum building. That day was one of the most emotional of all the talks I've been a part of.*

Carol shared her thoughts: *The UF event did a lot for me that day. It was the first time I met Gilbert King; he was so down to earth, a real easy person to talk with. I had never met a Pulitzer Prize winning author before and he was not at all like I thought he would be. He made me feel at ease, the butterflies in my stomach disappeared. It was also the first time I met the Shepard and Irvin families, and the first time I heard Henrietta Irvin speak about what had happened to her relative. Most of all, it was the very first time I met Josh in person and I felt as if I had known him all my life. I wanted to hold him and not let go. He became my inspiration after my father died. This was my Angel.*

That day, I felt that it was no longer me and Josh. My pain became the people in that room's pain, my quest for justice had become bigger than me and Josh. I felt sorry for Sam Harris, the nephew of Willis McCall. My father was right when he said, "what about the pain and embarrassment of the other family?" Sam's apology brought tears to my eyes and made me say to him, "it's alright, I forgive Willis McCall, and you don't have to apologize for him." I felt that the audience recognized racism still exists today and we need to start talking about it so that we can heal and not repeat that past.

Being on the panel at the UF law school gave the quest for justice more credibility. I felt like the Law School at the University of Florida raised the stature of the case, putting it squarely back into the legal arena. It allowed for the families' emotional aspect of the situation, but caught the attention of those who were motivated to look at the case as an injustice perpetuated by things other than the rule of law and justice. I saw this as a movement to move the case from a personal effort to one that impacted the state of Florida. Finally.

CAROL AND I MEET FOR THE FIRST TIME

7

Ben Polsky

 *"The youth of a nation are the trustees of posterity."*

Benjamin Disraeli

I MET ANOTHER PERSON IN DECEMBER WHO WOULD EMBRACE our cause in ways I couldn't have imagined. His name was Ben Polsky and he was in the fourth grade.

When I was Ben's age I had auditioned for a part in the Florida Children's Theatre's production of "The Prince and the Pauper", my first foray into acting. I almost chickened out when it came time to audition but, in the end, I was cast in the palace ensemble and got to wear a fancy costume. I was hooked on acting after that and for the next seven years (and subsequent summers) I performed in thirty plays, in roles ranging from minor roles to Prince Charming to Hamlet. FLCT was my home away from home and everyone there was my extended family. That's how I met Ben.

In the early days of our petition we had posted it everywhere, including the FLCT Facebook page, where Ben saw it. Ben's older brother happened to be reading Gilbert's book about the

"Devil in the Grove" for his AP English class and Ben had just completed a road trip to important civil rights sites in Atlanta and Alabama, which had a profound effect on him. When the chance to earn extra credit came up for school Ben decided to write a children's book about our quest to clear the Groveland Four.

I had my doubts that such a brutal story could be made suitable for children but Ben assured me it could be done. He started by interviewing me when I was home for the holidays and we agreed to meet in front of the children's theatre (of course). I remember how impressed I was by Ben's intelligent, thoughtful questions. Afterwards, I arranged for him to interview Carol by phone so he could start writing his book.

Ben and his mother Nancy drove to Gainesville in February for the UF forum and met the Groveland family members there, including Henrietta Irvin. While in Gainesville, Ben also interviewed Gilbert King. A short time later, Ben shared the story of the Groveland Four with his classmates. The following summer, Ben and his mom would finish writing his book, *Re-Righting History: The Groveland Boy*s and self-publish it on Amazon. Ben would gift copies of his book to the Groveland family members, Gilbert, Carol, and me. Ben was inspired by our project and we were equally inspired by his youthful energy and determination. As you will see, Ben's role in this story is far from over.

8

Politicians

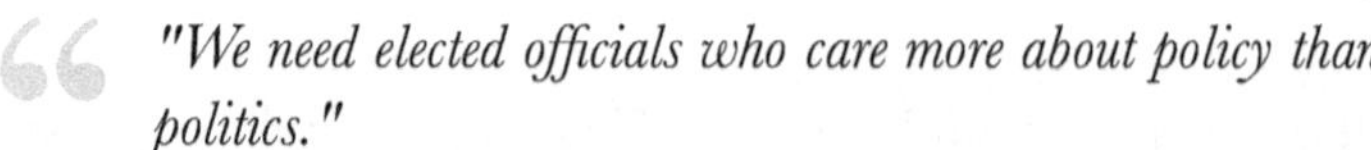

"We need elected officials who care more about policy than politics."

Christine Todd Whitman

FEBRUARY CONTINUED TO BE A BUSY MONTH FOR OUR CAUSE but I couldn't take the credit. Who could, you ask? Politicians, that's who.

As promised, Florida Senator Geraldine Thompson refiled her bill to exonerate the Groveland Four, but again failed to find a sponsor in the House.

Next, believe it or not, the City of Groveland jumped on board. Groveland Mayor Tim Loucks and the City Council, on their own, decided to issue a public apology to the families of the Groveland Four. And so, on February 16th 2016, more than a hundred people gathered at Groveland City Hall to hear that proclamation. A dozen family members of the Groveland Four attended, including Wade Greenlee, Charles Greenlee's brother. Senator Thompson, whose district it was, also attended, as did I. Carol couldn't make it as she was already planning to be at UF two days later for the panel. If you think Groveland was suddenly cured of all its racist tendencies, allow me to enlighten you. In the days leading up to the proclamation the mayor received anonymous threatening calls and demands to stop dredging up the past. Despite this, the mayor said most people were extremely supportive and he intended to meet with state officials to discuss exoneration in the near future.

He explained: "This is not the Groveland of 1949. What happened was a complete travesty of justice. I am hoping they are exonerated. It's important for the city to acknowledge what took place. For myself and for the city of Groveland, we do offer our sincere apologies. The biggest goal of the city of Groveland and south Lake County is ·to allow this to be healed. It's been ignored for 67 years. There comes a time when you can't ignore, should not ignore anything like this. It was very wrong in my opinion and it's time to face things and let the healing process begin. For years we've had our heads stuck in the sand wanting to ignore this, but this is the right thing to do. When I see something like this it's part of my responsibility to step up and see it's not right."

Senator Thompson added, "You and I here tonight, we are not responsible for what happened in 1949, but we are responsible for what happens on our watch. And on our watch, we want to acknowledge the racial and civil injustice that was done to members of the Groveland Four."

Wade Greenlee expressed his gratitude." It means a great deal to us if this happens and we can get a closure to this thing. To realize that the state admitted that they made a mistake and they did an injustice to these boys, that would mean a lot to these boys. My brother's gone on, and all those boys have gone on, but we still have family here. The family would like to see some closure. The family would like to see justice done.

An apology from the state would be fine. That's all we want. To admit there was a wrong done. I'm just sorry that he's not here to realize this."

Wade also attended the next public apology which came from Lake County and followed shortly thereafter.

At that event, Lake County Commissioner Sean Parks said: "It's the right thing to do. It was a terrible part of our history in Lake County. Maybe this will go toward making it right. There are things we can learn from our past. Lake County was not the best place to live in 1949 if you were African American. In fact, it was dangerous at times. These four men were wrongfully accused of a terrible crime. Angry mobs of people wanted to take justice into their own hands, convinced that these men committed a terrible crime simply because they were black. This dark chapter of Lake County's history has already been written--We cannot rewrite history but what we can do is write a new chapter in our history. We can become a force of unification. We can't reverse what happened, but we can propel forward our community in good spirit today, to exonerate these four men."

Groveland resident Ralph Morris, who attended, remarked: "This is a chance to not only exonerate and make right the names of the victims for their families but also for Lake County to stand up and show they don't support this type of action. This is an opportunity to say this is not who we are."

Charles Greenlee's son Thomas also attended the Lake County ceremony and said: "It's a huge step forward for our cause. I just want my father's name cleared. It was a different world then."

Not to be outdone, a third public apology came from the town of Mascotte, where some of the events had occurred.

Carol's reaction to the apologies: I was very surprised when the city of Groveland publicly apologized to the families. I did not know what to think. My uncle Wade attended both events. I was unable to attend but I received both Proclamations. I could not believe this was happening. Holding the Proclamations in my hand made it real. I had to wonder, what would my dad think? He would ask: is it helping anybody? Most of all my father would say: think about the other families, how are they feeling about this? Are you hurting them? Don't forget, (he would say) they have feelings too. The apology brought all this to mind. My father carried a lot on his shoulders: the protection and safety of our family, the protection, safety, and embarrassment of the other families, not to mention the pain he endured.

Gilbert's reaction to the apologies: To me, those events were all about building momentum. It was inspiring to see these communities taking action, but it was obvious that Josh had even bigger things in mind.

True to their word, Lake County officials did meet with Governor Rick Scott's staff in May of 2016 to plead the case for a pardon. It did not go well. Mayor Loucks brought up the Alabama pardon of the Scottsboro Boys, but Scott's staff members were unmoved. Scott's legal counsel said it was a "lengthy and drawn-out process to exonerate the men and he did not encourage it". He indicated that they might consider offering an apology. They never did.

9

More Publicity

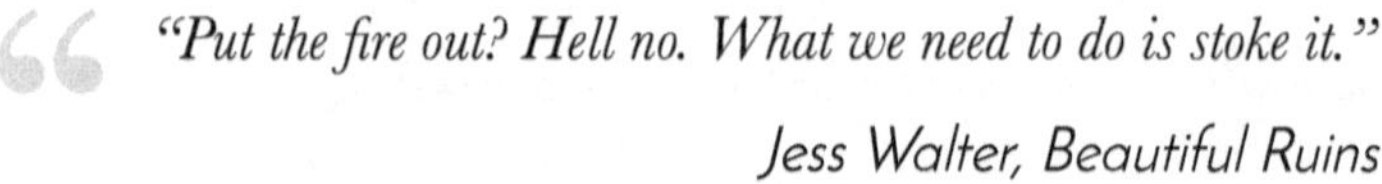

"Put the fire out? Hell no. What we need to do is stoke it."

Jess Walter, *Beautiful Ruins*

IN THE MONTHS FOLLOWING THE UF FORUM AND THE apologies by Groveland, Lake County, and Mascotte, not much happened and the number of petition signers slowed down considerably. We needed to shine another spotlight on our cause. But how? When I learned that one of my UF professors had done some freelance writing for Time Magazine my ears perked up. I gave her a pitch about our project. She listened politely and then said she had to decline. She thought it was a good cause, but her focus was on women's issues and she couldn't in good conscience write a story about a woman lying about being sexually assaulted without doing the research. Her reputation could be damaged. Seeing my disappointment she said she knew someone who might be interested, a journalist named Michael Stone who was based in Gainesville.

The good news was that Michael Stone *was* interested in writing a story. The bad news was that he didn't want to write about our petition, he wanted to write a piece on Gilbert King. The good news was that when he wrote the article about Gilbert he included a (very subtle) link to our petition in a sentence that said *concerned citizens* were "pushing for the state to apologize, exonerate and pardon the four". The bad news was the article only appeared in the online edition of Time. I didn't mind. As P.T. Barnum famously said, there's no such thing as bad publicity.

10

Margaret Grostefon

 *"A wise man turns chance into fortune."*

Thomas Fuller

HELP CAN COME FROM THE MOST UNEXPECTED PLACES. LET ME tell you about Margaret Grostefon. Actually, I don't know much about Margaret except she was there when we needed her.

My mother's friend Leslie Vien died unexpectedly in February of 2016 and my mother held a memorial at our house. Although she had known Leslie for twenty-five years my mother didn't know some of the people who came to pay their respects. That's because Leslie had such an eclectic group of friends--some she knew from Boston, others from work, others from various times of her life. Some shared Leslie's love of cats, others her love for the beach. My mom and Leslie liked to go to arthouse cinema together, drink wine and goof on the weird movies. The first time Leslie's friends all met was when they gathered around her hospital bed in the ICU. Margaret Grostefon was one of them.

In the months after the memorial my mom joked that she had inherited Leslie's friends. For starters, they had all become Facebook friends, including Margaret. Since my mom posted frequently about our Groveland project it made sense that Margaret would see it. A crusader for social justice, Margaret decided to spread the word about the Groveland Four. One day, while campaigning for Hillary Clinton, Margaret met a Democratic newcomer running for Florida Senate and she told him about the Groveland Four. She asked for his help if he won and he said yes. Margaret passed that information on to my mom who passed it on to me, which is why, on November 9th, the day after the election, I emailed that brand new legislator about sponsoring a bill to exonerate the Groveland Four. He said we could count on him. His name was Senator Gary Farmer.

11

More Politicians

"Hope is patience with the lamp lit."

Tertullian

I LIKED SENATOR FARMER RIGHT AWAY AND NOT JUST BECAUSE he had agreed to help us. He was personable and sincere and seemed like a person who got things done--even though he hadn't even started the job yet. Our exchanges quickly turned to strategy and I told him how the last two attempts at a bill had failed for lack of a sponsor in the House.

"So I took the liberty," I said, "of looking for potential sponsors. My first choice is Representative Bobby Dubose. He's from Broward and this is his kind of bill." My other choices were also Democrats from Broward but he stopped me there.

"Bobby DuBose is my friend," he said. "We've worked together before, I'll ask him."

I couldn't believe our good fortune. Bobby Dubose hadn't said yes but it looked promising. And since DuBose was starting his second term he would know his way around the process. The third try for a bill just had to be the charm.

Next step, alert the press! At the end of December I contacted Livi Stanford from The Daily Commercial who had written about the Groveland Four before, most recently about the apologies issued by Groveland and Lake County. Livi came through with a great article in which she recapped the tragic history of the Groveland Four and interviewed Senator Farmer, Mayor Loucks, Lake County Commissioner Sean Parks, Governor Scott's deputy press secretary (who had no update about the case and--spoiler alert--never would), Vivian Shepherd, Wade Greenlee, and Gilbert King. Whew, nice job, Livi!

To summarize the article, Mayor Loucks was disappointed with the lack of response from Governor Scott, but hopeful that Senator Farmer would be able to "light a fire". Commissioner Parks was disappointed that the men had not been cleared yet because Lake County wanted to put the past behind them. Senator Farmer found it to be a compelling case and was looking for a sponsor in the House. Wade and Vivian were hopeful and committed to keep fighting. Gilbert believed the legislation was critical because "posthumous exonerations will demonstrate that the state of Florida is committed to truth and justice in the past, present, and future."

A few days later, Representative Dubose joined the team and we were ready to roll.

Here are Carol's thoughts: *Getting Senator Gary Farmer to sponsor another bill was Josh's idea and I was in agreement. At this point I was all in. Josh had been very successful so far, Senator Farmer was new, so why not go straight to the Legislature. Senator Farmer was not part of the old crowd. Let's give it a try. I was very excited when Representative Bobby Dubose agreed to sponsor a companion bill.*

My thoughts: It didn't matter to us the race, gender, political affiliation, or district of our sponsoring legislators, we just wanted some help. Senator (now Representative) Geraldine Thompson, who had twice proposed a bill, is a black woman and a Democrat representing Orange County. Senator Farmer is white and Representative Dubose is black and both are Democrats representing Broward County, which was my home turf before I became a New Yorker. Several opinion columns have commented on how shameful it was that legislators from South Florida, and not Central Florida, were the ones to take on this racial injustice. I have to agree with that assessment, although Geraldine Thompson did try twice and I applaud her for that.

On January 1, 2017, true to his word, Senator Farmer sent us the first draft of the Resolution. It was in the form of a Resolution, not a Bill, because it wasn't intended to have the effect of law. It read, in part:

"That we hereby acknowledge that Charles Greenlee, Walter Irvin, Samuel Shepherd, and Ernest Thomas were the victims of gross injustices and that we apologize to the families of the Groveland Four for all of the aforementioned wrongs and deem the four men formally exonerated.

BE IT FURTHER RESOLVED that the Legislature urges the Governor and Cabinet to review the cases of Walter Irvin and Charles Greenlee and to grant Mr. Irvin and Mr. Greenlee pardons."

Carol and I were thrilled with the language--exonerate AND pardon!--it was like Christmas morning. Was the end of our journey in sight?

But Gilbert had reservations. On January 12th he emailed Senator Farmer the following: "One of my concerns with bringing this resolution is that the alleged victim, Norma

Padgett (now Norma Upshaw), is still alive, residing in Groveland, and has never recanted her story. I don't know what that could mean to this resolution, but I thought you should be aware of potential obstacles." He was more prescient than we knew.

On March 6th 2017, I felt like a proud parent watching the live feed of Senator Farmer as he introduced Senate Resolution 920 to the criminal justice committee in Tallahassee:

"All four gentlemen are deceased," he said, "but their families have had to live with these accusations or black mark on their family name for all this time. The exoneration is mainly symbolic, but to the families, it's huge. This is just a small token of what we can do as a state to right that wrong."

The next day, Representative Bobby Dubose introduced his identical resolution, House Resolution 631, to the House judiciary committee. The resolution passed through the Senate criminal justice committee. Next step was to get it passed through the Senate judiciary and rules committees and all three House committees before it could move to the Senate and House floors for a formal vote. If you ever sang along to Schoolhouse Rock's classic tune "I'm Just a Bill," the process is a lot like that, only on the State level.

Despite everyone's enthusiasm to deliver long-overdue justice, the Resolution stalled in the House after it cleared the judiciary committee in March. Representative Chris Sprowls from Pinellas County wasn't convinced, but changed his mind after a long chat with Carol about how this tragedy had shaped her life. Representative Larry Metz from Lake County had a problem with the Resolution's attempt to exonerate the Groveland Four. He argued that the legislature had no authority to exonerate the men as that power belonged to the judicial branch. Unfortunately, he was right.

After conducting research we learned there was no legal recourse for exoneration, only for a pardon. A person could be exonerated if he was convicted of a crime and later proven innocent through acquittal or dismissal of the charges. Because Charles Greenlee and Walter Irvin had both served time in prison (and had *not* been acquitted or had their case dismissed), the only legal remedy available was a posthumous pardon. Frustrated, Carol didn't want to settle for anything short of exoneration. She wasn't seeking a pardon, she said, because her father wasn't guilty of anything. She wanted his record wiped clean as if the conviction had never happened.

Only the Clemency Board, consisting of the Governor and two Cabinet members, had the authority to grant a full pardon and unconditionally release a person from punishment, forgiving guilt for any Florida convictions. As for the other two men, Ernest Thomas (who was killed within forty-eight hours of being accused) and Sam Shepherd (who was murdered by Sheriff McCall after the Supreme Court granted a retrial), it looked like they would get nothing. Apparently, they couldn't be pardoned or exonerated because neither one stood convicted of a crime at the time of his death. That was disappointing, especially for the Shepherd family. No one had been able to contact Ernest Thomas's relatives, so at least they hadn't gotten their hopes up.

The Resolution was revised and the final version was two pages longer than the first with more details about what had transpired. The prayer for exoneration had been removed and, instead, it urged the Governor and Clemency Board to expedite review of the case and grant full pardons for all four men--not just Charles Greenlee and Walter Irvin--something we had not thought possible. We had never gotten this far before, but we still had a long way to go.

Back To Ben

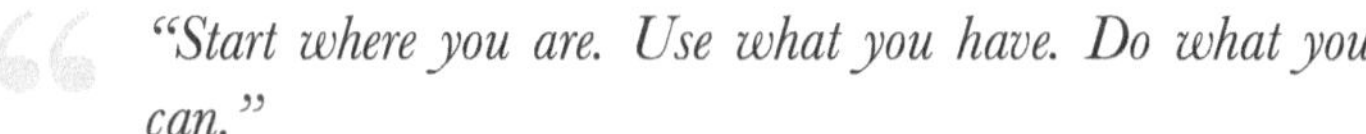

> *"Start where you are. Use what you have. Do what you can."*
>
> *Arthur Ashe*

IN FEBRUARY, AN FLCT MOM NAMED HOLLY JONES POSTED A request on the FLCT Facebook page for suggestions of non-fiction books that her daughter Kalia (age 12) could read for Black History Month. When Ben's mom Nancy saw the post she suggested Ben's book about The Groveland Four. Holly and Kalia borrowed Ben's copy and read it and then decided to start a Children's Book Club. Its stated purpose was "to keep our passionate, empathetic and naturally curious kiddos engaged in the world around them and empowered to make a difference. Books can be great resources for change-minded kids, helping them think about why and how they can be a force for good in the world. We will host quarterly book club meetings, on topics inspired by our kids and on the issues that affect us all. The goal is to then help facilitate the kids to take an associated action so that they can have an impact, large or small."

Snapping into action, Ben and Nancy asked for and received feedback from Gilbert King on their book, then hired an illustrator (my cousin Jake, a talented artist) and self-published the book on Amazon so the kids could get a few copies. Kalia and Holly scheduled a club meeting for February 26th to discuss the book. They also designed and printed postcards about the Groveland Four for the kids to fill out and send to their elected officials. Twenty-six kids (ranging from under ten to high school age) and some of their parents filled the room that night, excited about the events Holly had planned. My mom went for me (I was in New York) so she could answer a few questions. First, there was an in-depth discussion of the book with Ben about injustice, racism, and activism. Then, two laptops were set up side by side on the dining room table so the group could Skype with me and Carol, each of us on a different computer. They asked some great questions before turning the computers around so Carol and I could talk to each other. It was the first time Carol and I had spoken over Skype and we had fun. The kids got a kick out of it too. I was so impressed with everyone's interest in our project and in the story.

I heard Carol tell the kids how it was a Sunday the first time I had called her and how here it was another Sunday when they were calling her and that she couldn't believe how wonderful it all was and how they gave her so much hope for the future.

Carol and I signed off, but there was another surprise in store that night, one I heard about afterward.

In an amazing coincidence, it turned out Holly's husband Matt was friends with Bobby Dubose and had invited him to stop by. As the kids were writing their postcards, there was a knock on the door and Representative Dubose stepped in--a real, live legislator making house calls. Talk about democracy in action! In a moment that should have been captured on film the kids called Carol again over Skype and introduced her to Bobby Dubose. Carol was thrilled to meet one of the two men fighting for her cause in Tallahassee and Bobby Dubose seemed equally delighted to meet her. He told her he would make this his most important work that session.

At the book club meeting that night, one of the parents invited Ben and Nancy to be guest authors for Black History Month at the Broward County libraries. They happily accepted and printed more Groveland postcards so that people could send them to the governor to request a pardon. Together, Ben, Nancy, Holly and Kalia collected signed postcards at the library.

Over the next month, Ben and Nancy sent over two thousand postcards to every single legislator encouraging them to support the joint Resolution. They collected them at women's rallies and libraries, and Ben enlisted his entire middle school to write letters and postcards. They kept track of where the Resolution was in both the senate and house, called committee members, and sent copies of their book to each one as well as the committee chairs, along with handwritten letters.

Carol's thoughts: *Ben Polsky's children's book was brilliant. A stroke of genius to think of getting his school friends involved, sending specially designed postcards by his classmates to the Florida State Legislature. Ben's actions and advocacy helped move the Resolution in the Legislature.*

Kalia's thoughts: *I have always wanted to help people who were charged with something they didn't do. I actually thought I might want to become a criminal justice lawyer one day. As soon as I heard about the Groveland Four, I decided to make a book club to get more kids to read Ben's book in an effort to get them involved. Even though the Groveland Four are all dead, their families are alive, and I wanted us to come together to help right this wrong so they might begin to heal. Josh taught me that you should stand up even if it means standing alone.*

Twelve-year-old Elizabeth Abrams said: "Reading the book and meeting Carol made me feel like I could really take a stand –-at any age. The small act of writing letters made me feel empowered, because I knew I was helping to make a horrible event a tiny bit better."

THE CHILDREN'S BOOK CLUB

———

Each year, Representative Dubose held an event for Black History Month that was as well-planned as any theatrical production. The title of that year's event (held on March 20, 2017) was: "2017 Walk Through History, Through Our Eyes-- Remembering the Groveland Four" and he invited the Groveland families to attend (at his expense), including Carol, Wade, Vivian, Henrietta, and others. It was held at the Broward Center for the Performing Arts and was sponsored by the City of Fort Lauderdale, as well as some prestigious law firms. I couldn't attend since I was working in New York, but my parents went, as did Ben and Kalia, their parents, and Margaret Grostefon who had connected me to Gary Farmer. I heard there was a really nice reception with a buffet and open bar before the event.

After the invocation was given and the Negro National Anthem sung, a Spoken Word poet performed followed by a historical reenactment of a scene from the Groveland Four story, performed by members of the Kappa Alpha Psi Fraternity, of which Bobby Dubose was an alum. Next came a panel discussion that included Carol and her uncle Wade. All of the panelists received an award at the end and Ben and Kalia were called to the stage to present Carol with hers. The finale was a slide show of tragic events in local black history and a haunting performance of the song "Strange Fruit", which is about the lynching of black Americans, in case you are not familiar. Although it wasn't an upbeat way to end the night, it did ensure that this terrible history would not be forgotten.

Promises Kept

"True progress quietly and persistently moves along without notice."

Saint Francis de Sales

IN APRIL WE GOT THE CALL--COME TO TALLAHASSEE ON THE 18th, House Resolution 631 is scheduled for a vote. Although Senator Farmer tried to schedule the Senate vote on his resolution for the same day, it didn't come together and in the end it didn't matter. The level of drama and expectation couldn't have been any higher than it already was.

I flew in from New York, Carol, her brother Thomas and his son drove in from Tennessee, stopping to pick up their Uncle Wade in Jacksonville on the way; Vivian Shepherd drove in from Orlando, my mom, Ben and Nancy Polsky, Kalia Jones and her parents, Holly and Matt, came from south Florida, and other Shepherd and Irvin family members came too. Sadly, Henrietta Irvin couldn't make the trip from Miami, but Gilbert King was there. He wouldn't have missed it for the world.

A press conference was held before the vote and it was everything I could have hoped for--specifically, lots of press and a chance for everyone to speak. Bobby Dubose kicked it off by saying it was an historic day and that the injustice done to the Groveland Four was hard to put into words. He acknowledged that the resolution couldn't erase the pain but hoped that their apology could provide closure for the families.

Next, Gary Farmer said he was honored to sponsor this meaningful resolution which recognized the mistakes that were made and hoped it would give some peace and closure to the families. He acknowledged that the pain and heartbreak of these wrongful accusations were a dark chapter in our history and said he was proud to be part of this group. Paraphrasing Martin Luther King Jr., he said the moral arc of the universe bends toward Tallahassee today and shines on us.

House Speaker Corcoran briefly spoke about how this was a dark cloud over our history and that when those in positions of leadership don't seek truth and justice the depth of depravity is limitless.

House Chair Sprowls spoke about how it was not only the men but also their families who had suffered from this grave injustice and he had realized this after speaking with Carol Greenlee.

Florida Senator Geraldine Thompson spoke next. I was glad she had been invited since she had tried to sponsor a bill twice. Senator Thompson explained how she had taken a step to acknowledge this injustice years before and compared the quest to a relay race in which she had passed the baton to Bobby Dubose and Gary Farmer.

And then Carol, my personal favorite, spoke:

"This is a glorious day. I feel today the tears are hard to hold back but today the tears are tears of joy and I want to thank all of you for releasing my family from prison, for releasing my nieces, my son, my brothers, from the dark cloud, the shame and the stigma that have been put upon them and for releasing me after 67 years. I was the child, I was the baby my father went to Groveland to support back in 1949 and today I feel free. I feel like I can talk about it, I feel like I can sit down with my nieces and nephews and brothers and tell the story that at my age 40, my father told me. Thank you, State of Florida, House of Representatives, thank you, Senator, for releasing the Greenlee family. God bless you."

With a hug, Carol turned the podium over to Jeannette Shepherd Tatum. Shaking with emotion, Jeannette shared how in 2004 she had been exploring her family tree and was shocked to learn through an internet search that her uncle, Sam Shepherd, was one of the Groveland Four. She found a book about it, *The Groveland Four: The Sad Saga of a Legal Lynching*, and reached out to the author, Gary Corsair, to learn more. She read the book and cried and read some more until she finally got through it.

"This has been a long time coming," she said, "and we so appreciate all you have done so far. My dad's little brother was only thirteen or fourteen when all this happened and it was traumatic for him. It was my grandparents' house they (the KKK) burned down and my grandparents had to run. My dad, his brothers and sisters never talk about this. On behalf of the Shepherd family I thank you for all of the love and support you have given us."

Gilbert took the podium next: "Today marks a willingness to recognize and confront a grave injustice. Sadly, for the families of the Groveland Boys this bill cannot alter the tragic course of history but it does show how we, as Americans, can respond to our past, to acknowledge a shameful part of our history and to confront it, rather than sweeping it under the rug and moving on without conversation. Josh Venkataraman was a student at the University of Florida last year when he studied this story in a history class. He was so moved by the injustice he began to contact the families, many of whom are here today. He started a petition, getting thousands of signatures; he wrote to representatives, state senators, to the media, he was his own grassroots movement. Josh is a young American who did not want to see this injustice swept under the rug; he was moved to take action. It is that spirit of bipartisan action that should be an inspiration to all of us today."

Then Ben Polsky was called and said he wrote his book after learning about the Groveland Four. He explained that after meeting the families the cause became very personal to him and he thanked everyone.

It was my turn next. "When I first started this two years ago, I didn't expect all of this and I think what I've learned is that even though it is a cliché it does take a village. All of these people here surrounding me are the people that made this happen and helped to rewrite history and change this wrong that was done in our state. We're making our state a better place, we're getting rid of this scar that haunted our state. I want to thank Representative Dubose, Senator Farmer, everyone else standing here because it really does take a spark to get this big fire moving and make change happen."

Representative Dubose then recognized his co-primary sponsor, a Republican named Jason Fischer, and called upon Larry Metz, the Representative whose district included Groveland and the person who had twice declined to support Geraldine Thompson's bill. Representative Metz said he read Gilbert's book and because the record showed grave injustices had occurred, he agreed that this was an appropriate action to take. In his closing statement, Bobby Dubose said the State of Florida was wrong and we're sorry.

Bobby Dubose: What inspired me to sponsor this resolution was the injustice these young men faced. Getting closure for their respective families was the driving force for me and I sincerely believed something fruitful would come of it. On a personal level, I was raising black boys that were about the same age as the Groveland Four so their ordeal resonated with me deeply. Senator Farmer and I actively worked in both chambers to garner support on the language. Working on this project strengthened our work relationship and friendship. Our biggest obstacle was the overwhelming pushback from Republican leadership on both fronts.

THAT'S ME, SPEAKING AT THE PRESS CONFERENCE

Kalia's thoughts on her trip to Tallahassee: *I met many family members of the Groveland Four and listened to their stories. I was inspired by Ms. Carol Greenlee because she could have been angry and bitter, but instead she was just so full of love, her story was an inspiration. I learned from many of the family members that even when you're hurting you can be a source of happiness for each other and come together.*

I got to visit the capitol! I learned how every person has a role to play and how important it is to work together. I learned that when voting on an issue everyone had buttons on their desk- either Yes or No. When the voting happens each person's name shows up on the screen with their vote. It filled me with so much happiness to watch the screen fill up with all Yes votes to pardon the Groveland Four! I was hoping it would happen but nothing can describe how happy I was when it actually happened. We were all rejoicing. It felt so amazing to be sitting with the family when they received their formal apologies! I was trying to stay calm but I was so excited I was on the verge of jumping in the air with joy!

I had many people come up to me in the Capitol building to say they had received loads of postcards from young people, including me, and that they hung them in their offices. I felt so happy to be a part of this. It all started with Josh and his petition which inspired us all to come together and join forces (Ben Polsky's book, the book club, all of the postcards etc.). I think without everyone's efforts it wouldn't have been possible.

Ben's thoughts: *In April 2017 we got the call to go to Tallahassee for the big*

vote. When we arrived, imagine my surprise that all these politicians knew my book and wanted to take pictures with me! Turns out Representative Dubose and Senator Farmer got copies for every legislator!

That day as we sat in the House galley for the vote, Carol held my hand. At the end she told me it was five years ago to the day her father had passed away; she said I believe he's resting in peace now. Wow.

I learned politicians are people just like us. They feel proud of themselves when they make good choices. There was a real sense of joy and goodwill among all the Democrats and Republicans that day.

I learned some technical things about the process, like the role of the legislature versus that of the governor; I learned a really valuable lesson from Representative Dubose and Senator Farmer to seek out allies across the aisle. Without bipartisan co-sponsorship, I don't think it would've passed unanimously. I also learned government can work. We had a grassroots campaign to raise awareness and it worked.

Josh was Facetiming with Miss Henrietta in the row in the front of me. I kept looking at her face, imagining what she must feel. Carol was squeezing my hand harder and harder. Seeing the board change with all the lights voting Yay was so much more than expected. But unanimous yes votes and co-sponsorship was more than I could have ever imagined

————

My thoughts: *Sitting high up in the gallery we had a bird's eye view of the entire room. My mom and I were in the front row and as much as I wanted to savor every minute of the process, it was a challenge. Not only did I want to watch the action, I also wanted to crane my neck to watch Carol's reaction. That wasn't an option because I had promised Henrietta Irvin I would Facetime with her so she could watch the proceedings in real time. Unfortunately, I kept losing her and had to call back several times. In the meantime, Vivian Shepherd was texting me repeatedly which seemed odd until I realized she wasn't in the gallery with us. Poor Vivian- -after driving from Orlando to Tallahassee she had gone to buy some food and gotten locked out of the hearing. Once it started, she was not permitted to enter and she was devastated.*

Despite all these distractions, when the yes votes started pouring in from the floor my heart soared. It was simply amazing! But the best was yet to come. After the voting was over and the resolution passed the entire House of Representatives turned to face the gallery, looked up and issued a heart-felt apology to the families of the Groveland Four. It was like something out of a movie, a poignant, joyful moment and I was a part of it. We all were.

Later, Bobby Dubose hosted a reception in another room to celebrate. After he welcomed everyone with a few words he handed the microphone to Vivian so she could participate in this historic event she had only been able to watch on a screen from outside the room. It was a thoughtful gesture and one which she appreciated.

————

The apology to the Groveland Four was not the only one offered that day and I would be remiss if I didn't include the other one here. The House members spent a lot of time discussing a horrific part of Florida history that I had never heard of: The Florida School for Boys, also known as the Arthur G. Dozier School for Boys, a reform school operated by the state in the town of Marianna from January 1900 through June 2011. For a time, it was the largest juvenile reform institution in the country.

Here is the Wikipedia summary: Throughout its 111-year history, the school gained a reputation for abuse, beatings, rapes, torture, and even murder of students by staff. Despite periodic investigations, changes of leadership, and promises to improve, the allegations of cruelty and abuse continued. After the school failed a state inspection in 2009, the governor ordered a full investigation. Many of the historic and recent allegations of abuse and violence were confirmed by separate investigations by the Florida Department of Law Enforcement in 2010, and by the Civil Rights Division of the United States Department of Justice in 2011. State authorities closed the school permanently in June 2011. At the time of its closure, it was a part of the Florida Department of Juvenile Justice.

Because of questions about the number of deaths at the school and a high number of unmarked graves, the state authorized a forensic anthropology survey by University of South Florida in 2012. They identified 55 burials on the grounds, most outside the cemetery, and documented nearly 100 deaths at the school. The state said it did not have authority to allow exhumation of graves, which would permit determination of cause of death and identification of remains. (In addition it wanted to sell land on the property.) A family member of a student who died at the school in 1934, and who wanted to reinter his remains, filed suit and gained an injunction against the state's moving ahead with the sale before remains could be exhumed and identified. The state responded to the court injunction and authorized more work by a multi-disciplinary team from the University of South Florida, including exhumations. In January 2016, the USF team issued its final report, having made seven DNA matches and 14 presumptive identifications of remains. They will continue to work on identification.

In 2019, during preliminary survey work for a pollution clean-up, a further 27 suspected graves were identified by ground penetrating radar. Many people, including former detainees, believe that over 100 bodies were buried on the schools grounds, and that further investigating should be done until all the remains have been identified and cared for.

In March 2014, Governor Rick Scott signed a bill authorizing up to $7,500 per burial for those families who wanted to reinter the remains of relatives identified in unmarked graves at the Florida School for Boys. This followed the University of South Florida's report in January, which said they had been able to make matches of 21 sets of remains to known families. In addition, the bill proposes creating a task force to establish a memorial, "as well as deciding how to handle the remains of bodies that have yet to be identified or claimed by families."

On April 26, 2017, the state held a formal ceremony with families and survivors to apologize for the abuses of children at the school. Both houses of the legislature passed resolutions supporting the apology. Some two dozen men stood as their names were called. A proposed House bill would fund two memorials to be built in Tallahassee and in Marianna, reburial of remains, and provide some kind of restitution to victims. The Senate said it would consider it. *As of April, 2019, it had not passed.* A spokesman for the White House Boys (an organized group of survivors of the Dozier School) said they did not want any remains reburied on the grounds of the school or even in the county, as they believed local people were complicit in what went on there.

———

Carol's closing comment that day: *Today, a part of it is forgiveness. And my father would feel good about that. This means that something positive has come out of something so wrong and so negative and so bad.*

I didn't disagree, but Florida still had a lot of work to do to make amends for its past.

Post-Resolution

> *"A little more persistence, a little more effort, and what seemed hopeless failure may turn to glorious success."*
>
> *Elbert Hubbard*

THE JOINT RESOLUTION PASSED AND WE WERE HAPPY, believing it was a significant step towards a pardon. After all, it made the front page of both the Sun-Sentinel and the Miami Herald and even received a write up in the Washington Post. The Florida Legislature had taken a stand, publicly urging the Governor and Clemency Board to expedite a review and grant full pardons to the men. Surely that meant something.

One person who was unimpressed by the news was Leonard Pitts Jr. In his column dated May 2, 2017 he enumerated the many atrocities the Groveland Four had suffered (including severe beatings and two of them being shot dead) before concluding that Florida's apology to four black men after seventy years fell far short of being justice. While he agreed that credit was due the lawmakers who had shepherded the bills through, and to me and Carol for our efforts, he said that in a case where right and wrong were so jarringly clear, it shouldn't take nearly a lifetime to get it. He pointed out that before we should feel good about how enlightened we've become, we needed to remember what happened to Trayvon Martin and to other young black men. He said enlightenment required standing up to injustice in the moment and not just apologizing for it seventy years after the fact. He was right, of course.

Soon after the Resolution passed, Governor Scott was asked at a press conference about the status of a pardon for the Groveland Four and appeared to have no idea who they were. His office later issued a statement that they were aware of the Groveland Four case and that any application for clemency would be reviewed by the Clemency Board (which included the governor).

That's when I realized no one had filed an application for clemency! I remembered discussing it with Gilbert a while back and that he had planned to ask a lawyer friend to do it. When I reached out Gilbert was apologetic but said his friend hadn't been able to help. I decided to take a crack at it myself. I'd have to file one for Charles Greenlee and another for Walter Irvin, the two men who had been convicted and served time.

The application for clemency was available online and consisted of just one page. It seemed pretty straightforward but there were many questions I couldn't answer--starting with the driver's license number and social security number of the person seeking a pardon. It only got worse from there, requiring a list of each conviction and the court documents, followed by court date, convicted/date sentenced, date sentence was completed, and signature. The icing on the cake was the requirement that I attach a *certified* copy of the following for EACH felony conviction: charging indictment information; judgment; and felony conviction: charging indictment information; judgment; and sentence/community control/probation order.

This was going to be a challenge. Carol could provide her father's birthdate and Social Security number and Henrietta knew her brother Walter's birthdate, but that wasn't nearly enough. And how, pray tell, was I supposed to get certified documents from court cases over sixty-five years old? I contacted the Clerk of Court in Lake County who directed me to the archives department where I tried to order the records. They said they would try but seriously doubted the records still existed. Gilbert didn't have them either. Then I hit the jackpot, sort of. Walter Irvin's conviction (but not Charles Greenlee's) had been appealed to the U.S. Supreme Court by Thurgood Marshall and the opinion could be found online under *Shepherd v. Florida (1951)*.

After filling in as many blanks as I could and exploring every option I called Adam Putnam's office. As Agriculture Commissioner he was one of the four members of the Clemency Board. When I explained my dilemma to Kyle Troop, Putnam's clemency attorney, he was helpful. He advised me to go ahead and file what I had and to ask for expedited processing, which I did. On June 5th, 2017, I emailed the Clemency Board to confirm that my application had been received. After that, I called Kyle every so often to ask if my petition would be on the next meeting's agenda. The answer was always no. To give you some perspective, the Clemency Board was tasked with considering pardons and restoration of rights and had at least a ten year backlog, which was by design. My only hope was that the Joint Resolution carried some weight and that all the publicity would push our case to the front of the line. Eventually, I stopped calling Kyle, I mean, what was the point?

I needed somebody new to pester so I started emailing House Speaker Richard Corcoran. Porsche Knight, his Scheduler and Logistics Coordinator, responded and we corresponded from September through February with me asking for help and her promising to look into it. In February she stopped responding altogether.

In the meantime, Ben and Kalia, full of boundless energy and optimism, jumped back into action. Ben's teachers embraced the teachable moment in the spring of 2018 and assigned Ben's book as a reading assignment to his class at Seminole Middle School. The kids then wrote dozens of letter to the Clemency Board members requesting an expedited pardon.

Kalia said: We continued to send postcards to the entire board, urging them to honor the unanimous votes in the state Senate and House. I hoped that being kids would help us to touch something deep in these people's hearts so that they would grant the pardon.

Gilbert was more cautious. He was braced for the reality that although momentum was building, there was a very good chance that everything would grind to a halt due to political and bureaucratic machinations. But he never thought it was over. He just began to expect a delayed crawl toward justice.

Bobby Dubose was under the impression that once the resolution passed, Governor Scott would do his part and pardon the men. He thought that the application to the Clemency Board had been submitted prior to the Resolution and was surprised to learn that this wasn't the case.

I soon realized that filing the application wouldn't change a thing. Not for quite some time.

———————————————

15

The Press Presses On

———————————————

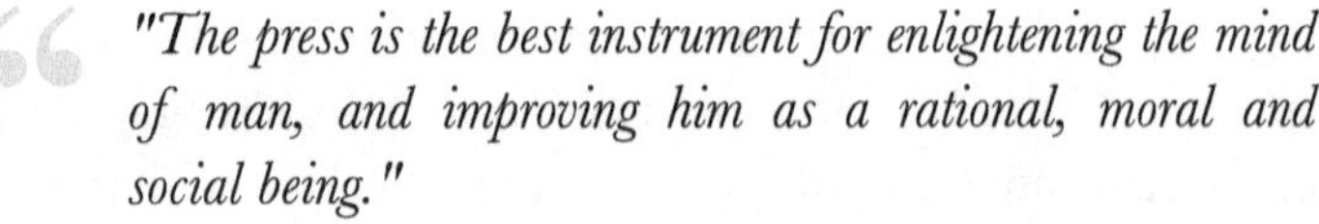

> *"The press is the best instrument for enlightening the mind of man, and improving him as a rational, moral and social being."*
>
> *Thomas Jefferson*

YOU MAY BE WONDERING WHETHER THE PRESS HAD MOVED ON from this story. Could you blame them if they had? With so much happening in the country, who had time for a seventy year old tale of racial injustice? Scott Powers, that's who. An Orlando journalist, Scott Powers wrote four articles about our case from November 2017 through December 2018. The first one, published on the Orlando-Rising website on November 20, 2017 was titled "Where are the Groveland Four Pardons? Their Story Continues in Silence." There, Powers provided a brief history of the case and explained how the request for pardons had "vanished into bureaucracy". He reported that requests for status to the Governor's office had garnered no response. He included a statement by Kelly Corder, director for communications for the Florida Commission on Offender Review, that investigations are processed in the order they were received and that as of November 1, 2017 there were 22,376 pending clemency cases. In light of that bad news, he compared our case to the last scene in *Raiders of the Lost Ark*. You know, the one where the Ark of the Covenant is wheeled into an enormous warehouse, never to be seen again?

Less than ten days later, Scott Powers wrote another article for Orlando-Rising: "Rick Scott's Office: Governor is aware of Groveland Four Case, reviewing all options". It dealt with how Governor Scott had declined to talk about the posthumous pardons being sought for the Groveland Four at a press conference but, hours later, said he was aware of the case and reviewing options. Powers reiterated the tragic story and how it had finally been brought to light. Personally, I think Scott Powers should change his byline to Scott "Speaking Truth to Power", a name he truly lives up to.

———

Aside from these news stories, things were happening behind the scenes that I was unaware of. Senator Gary Farmer, equally frustrated with the lack of progress, had recruited the help of Chris Hand, a Florida attorney (and UF Gator) with a long history of public and civic service. Hand had served as speechwriter, campaign press secretary, and Senate press secretary for former U.S. Senator Bob Graham and had also co-authored a book with the Senator: *America, the Owner's Manual: You Can Fight City Hall—and Win.*

My first contact with Chris was on March 6, 2018 when, to my surprise, he sent me an email thanking me for my citizen leadership on behalf of the Groveland Four. He went on to say that he and a group of influential Florida attorneys wanted to support my efforts by persuading at least one member of the State Clemency Board to order an expedited review of the Groveland Four pardon applications and at least three members to support granting pardons. He also had a plan to engage with the media to build awareness about the Groveland Four. In fact, Chris had already taken action in the form of a letter, which he had attached to the email. Addressed to the Clemency Board, it laid out the case for a pardon nearly a year after the unanimous Joint Resolution had passed and nine months after I had filed the pardon applications. He also offered to meet with the Board in Tallahassee to discuss the case. The letter was signed by thirty-three attorneys. Good work, Chris!

If you think that was the end of our quest and that the Clemency Board jumped right on it, think again. What they did was continue to ignore the case and hope it would go away. They were getting good at that.

Chris's plan to engage the media entailed seeking pro bono services from Edelman Orlando, a branch of a global marketing and communications firm. As a result of Edelman's efforts, another article appeared in the Orlando Sentinel on September 7, 2018. The journalist, Lauren Ritchie, again provided the background of the case and then explained the efforts made by the Edelman group while shaming the Clemency Board for their inaction. The article also supplied a link for readers to who wanted to contact the Clemency Board and demand justice for the Groveland Four.

Three days later, our old friend Scott Powers was back. In an article written for *Florida Politics*, he discussed the latest developments in the Groveland Four case, specifically, that December 5th would be the last meeting of the Clemency Board before the next election and that, just like with the five prior meetings, the pardons were not on the agenda. The Board members had never publicly said whether they had any intention of considering the pardons and their silence spoke volumes.

It wasn't all bad news though. Powers reported that all four Democratic Florida Cabinet nominees had pledged to act swiftly on behalf of the Groveland Four if elected. Unsurprisingly, the Republican nominees had declined to comment. The article mentioned the coalition pushing for the pardon which included Edelman Orlando, the family members, Gilbert, me, and Carol. It was a powerful piece that highlighted the anguish of the families. It ended with a quote by the spokesman for Andrew Gillum, the Democratic gubernatorial nominee, saying that the Groveland Four and their families deserved closure. Amen to that.

Two months later, on December 2, 2018, the Editorial Board of the Tallahassee Democrat issued an opinion piece that the Clemency Board must act now and pardon the Groveland Four. Although they laid the shame on pretty thick, the Clemency Board remained immune.

The very next day, Scott Powers reported in Florida Politics that the final meeting of the Clemency Board had been postponed due to the death of President George H.W. Bush, but said there was still a chance for a pardon to happen. He quoted Chris Hand who explained that, according to the Florida clemency rules, the Governor has unfettered discretion to grant at any time, for any reason, full pardons with the support of two other Cabinet members. Should that not occur, Powers went on, it would be left to the incoming Cabinet which had but one member who supported full and swift pardons: Democrat Nikki Fried, newly elected Secretary of Agriculture.

Popular At Last

 *"The secret of success is to be ready when your opportunity comes."*

Benjamin Disraeli

HAVE YOU EVER BEEN FIRST PICK FOR A TEAM SPORT AND had people fight over you? Me neither, but I think I know how it feels. Somehow, we had reached a tipping point in our journey and didn't even realize it. Just two weeks later--two weeks!--the Groveland Four had become a cause célèbre, the most popular kid at the party, and we owed it all to Nikki Fried (and Chris Hand, who had made her an ally).

On December 17, 2018, in an article for the Herald/Times, Tallahassee Bureau, Lawrence Mower reported that Nikki Fried planned to move to pardon the Groveland Four during the first meeting of the Cabinet. She also issued a statement: "We must look to correct this grave injustice and denounce the abuses of the past. I hope to convince my colleagues that a pardon is the right and just decision." In other words, she would force a vote on the pardons. In the same article, incoming Attorney General, Ashley Moody said she was very interested in a pardon and that it would be one of the first things she looked at.

Two days later, our old friend Scott Powers was back, this time with some good news: another member of the incoming Cabinet was on board, Jimmy Patronis. Patronis, Florida's Chief Financial Officer was the only current Cabinet member who would be returning.

"The time to do the right thing is now," Patronis said. "I'm ready to put it on the agenda and have it heard." His letter also instructed the Office of Executive Clemency to immediately begin conducting their clemency report.

Carol's reaction was enthusiastic to say the least: "Oh, Lord, thank you, Jesus! Thank you! Thank you! Thank you!"

I contacted Henriettta Irvin, Walter's sister, to tell her and she said it was wonderful news, that she had been waiting her whole life for this.

As if that weren't surprising enough, Florida Republican Senator Marco Rubio (who had *never, ever* said a word about the Groveland case before) took to the floor of the U.S. Senate to call for pardons. He echoed Patronis: "It is time to do the right thing for the Groveland Four."

Two days later, Governor-elect Ron DeSantis announced he would make the issue of a pardon a priority for the first Cabinet meeting in January.

What in the world was happening? Why did they steal Nikki Fried's thunder? It's not like they didn't have seventy years to take action. The answer is simple--Fried's plan to force a vote meant that Republican Cabinet members would have to go on record. If they voted NO to a pardon they would be the villains and Nikki would be the hero, so they pretended they

always planned to do the right thing. But history doesn't lie--
they had seven Clemency Board meetings to consider a
pardon and never even put it on the agenda, despite hundreds
of letters, extensive news coverage and shaming, and fervent
pleas from the families.

Chris Hand summed it up nicely: "Justice for the Groveland
Four has seen more progress this month than at any time since
the Florida Legislature unanimously requested a pardon in
April 2017."

To Pardon Or Not To Pardon

"You take it on faith, you take it to the heart, the waiting is the hardest part."

Tom Petty

WHEN I AWOKE ON FRIDAY, JANUARY 4TH, I DIDN'T KNOW IT would be a momentous day. The holidays were over and I was back in New York City trying to stay warm. I worked all morning and when my phone rang in the afternoon it caught me by surprise. It was Senator Farmer calling with big news: a hearing had been scheduled for the following Friday in Tallahassee and Jimmy Patronis was the driving force behind it. We were both excited at the prospect and I promised to book my ticket right away. Immediately after that an email appeared in my in-box:

Mr. Venkataraman,

As the interested party who filed an application for clemency for Mr. Walter Irvin and Mr. Charles Lorenza Greenlee, I wish to advise you that the Florida Board of Executive Clemency will be discussing the Groveland Four request. This will occur after the scheduled Cabinet meeting on Friday, January 11, which commences at 9:00 a.m.

The Cabinet meeting can also be viewed live on the FL Channel at https://thefloridachannel.org/. If you have any questions, please advise. Also, please acknowledge receipt of this email.

Julia McCall, CPM
Coordinator Office of Executive Clemency
Florida Commission on Offender Review

I didn't do much work the rest of the day; I was too busy working the phones. I called Gilbert, Carol, and Henrietta. It was a little sad because Henrietta definitely didn't remember me, but she still processed the information. I also called my parents and my brother Scott to share the good news. My parents offered to drive up from Fort Lauderdale for the hearing and change their vacation plans to work it in. I was cautiously optimistic although I knew it wasn't a done deal. Carol was less pleased than I thought she would be.

*Carol's response: My first call came from Chris Hand. He said the Clemency Board was going to **review** the Groveland Four case. My reaction was, we have reviewed this case for 70 years I am sick and tired of just reviewing the case. They can do that without me. I was very tempted not to make the trip. Then Josh called, I cannot say NO to Josh. So I tried to be excited and show up. I had no idea that I would have to speak to the Board.*

Three days before the hearing, after I'd already bought a plane ticket, Chris Hand called to say he had heard the hearing would be just a discussion and that they probably wouldn't vote on it until the next session in March. I now understood why Carol had no faith in the system. The only thing she could count on was being disappointed.

———

On Thursday, January 10th, the day before the hearing, another apology came from an unexpected quarter, the Orlando Sentinel Editorial Board. I wondered why they felt the need to apologize, but they explained it in great detail.

"We're sorry for the Orlando Sentinel's role in this injustice. We're sorry that the newspaper at the time did between little and nothing to seek the truth. We're sorry that our coverage of the event and its aftermath lent credibility to the cover-up and the official, racist narrative.

We're sorry that reporters and editors failed in our duty to our readers, to the community and to the Groveland Four and their families. The newspaper, then called the Orlando Morning Sentinel, published many stories about the incident and the aftermath."

They went on to say that the story had many more ugly twists and turns, marked by lies, cover-ups and injustice than the official version, but that the paper had chosen to inflame the public instead by publishing a cartoon on the front page with four empty electric chairs labeled *The Lake County Tragedy* and *The Supreme Penalty*.

They provided other examples of their inflammatory articles and editorials. They explained that the Sentinel's electric chairs cartoon was cited in the U.S. Supreme Court decision overturning the convictions of Shepherd and Irvin as one of the factors that should have led to a change in venue.

Although this kind of coverage would not happen today, they said, it does not excuse them from taking responsibility for that past coverage and they asked for the public's pardon.

———

January 11, 2019 was a day of reckoning seventy years in the making. It was incredible that by just reading a book for school I found myself in Florida's State Capitol four years later. I had flown in from New York the night before and was now rushing to meet Carol and my parents before the hearing started. I hoped this wasn't an exercise in futility but, like most things, it was out of my control.

Carol had driven in from Tennessee with her brother and nephew and they were already inside the chambers along with other Groveland family members, including Wade Greenlee, Charles's brother. Of course, Gilbert King was there, as were Senator Farmer, Representative Dubose and Representative Geraldine Thompson.

After hugs all around, we settled into our seats. Suddenly, a buzz went through the packed house as an elderly woman in a wheelchair was pushed into the room flanked by her family. It was Norma Padgett! After nearly seventy years of silence the accuser of the Groveland Four had come to speak. She wouldn't be the only one with a chance to speak--Chris Hand and Senator Farmer informed us that a vote was, in fact, going to happen and that each of us would have an opportunity to speak. I was caught off guard because all week we had been told it wasn't happening and so we weren't prepared, but I knew we would manage. I was feeling upbeat because we had never gotten this far before. I didn't believe the Board would convene with so much fanfare if they weren't planning to vote yes--especially in light of what they had said in the past few weeks--but once Norma showed up, my confidence wavered.

Governor Ron DeSantis called the Executive Clemency Board meeting to order and addressed the crowd:

"We are here today to discuss the cases of Mr. Charles Greenlee, Mr. Walter Irvin, Mr. Samuel Shepherd, and Mr. Ernest Thomas, collectively known as the Groveland Four. This case is a priority for me and several of my fellow board members. We will be addressing a full pardon, a determination of innocence or guilt is not a prerequisite for granting clemency. These are extraordinary circumstances and we not follow the protocol. I hope today through thoughtful and purposeful discussion we can find a resolution and bring long-awaited peace to everyone who was impacted by this tragedy 70 years ago. That's a long time. First, we will hear testimony of those in favor of granting the pardon."

Carol spoke first: "I'm the daughter of Charles Greenlee and I appreciate the opportunity to address the Board this morning. My father is deceased, he died in 2012 and I would ask you to grant the pardon. There have been many investigations and documents supporting the facts that my father wasn't even in the area when the incidents occurred. He was incarcerated at the time the accident occurred. I also know there are facts to prove the other three were innocent, from the FBI reports and other investigations. Those ruled out that these gentlemen were involved. I ask you this morning to look at the facts that have been presented to you from several individuals, including the FBI reports that show that they were not guilty. I was the individual that my father went to Groveland to get a job to support. I asked my father when I was forty years old what happened. He said I knew more about it than he did. The first time he laid eyes on these individuals was in the courtroom.

My father was not there. He was accused, put in jail, tortured for something he did not do. I ask you today to please pardon my father and the other men."

Carol's brother Thomas was next: "My brother and I had to deal with the aftermath of a sixteen-year-old taken for something he did not do, did not understand. He was taken to prison and the people around the prison wanted him released so they could lynch him. He was incarcerated for twelve years for something he did not do. He was beaten so bad, a sixteen-year-old child who had done nothing more than try to take care of his responsibility, his daughter. What hurt him the most was that he was not there for his daughter. You put him in a situation where you not only affected him but the whole family. He had every reason to be angry, but he was not. My father was the greatest man I ever met."

Gilbert spoke next: "My name is Gilbert King and I'm the author of *Devil in the Grove* which discusses this case to quite an extent. Thank you for allowing me to speak on behalf of the families. In 1949, four young black men were powerless to defend themselves from the brutality of a Lake County sheriff and his deputies, they were powerless to fight back against a corrupt prosecutor and judge, and they were powerless to defend themselves against explosive accusations leveled against them by a seventeen-year-old white woman in the Jim Crow South. When we look back at the case of the Groveland Four, a case that led to four people being killed, including two of the accused, it's a system we barely recognize as a criminal justice system. Seventy years is a long time ago. There was manufactured evidence, perjury, witnesses being hidden from the defense, and prosecutorial misconduct that was rampant throughout this case.

Even with the great Thurgood Marshall representing the Groveland Four, they were no match for a state attorney bent on vengeance, on a first name basis with twelve white male jurors in Lake County. In 2017, the Florida legislature, in a strong bi-partisan effort, voted unanimously to apologize, in the both the House and the senate, to apologize to the families of the Groveland Four and to recommend posthumous exonerations be given to amend for this grave injustice.

Seventy years is a long time but it's not ancient history as we are well aware today. These young black men may have been powerless to defend themselves in 1949 but there is a great deal of exculpatory evidence that was hidden from their lawyers seventy years ago. Evidence we have today thanks to FBI files that have been since unsealed. The Groveland Four were denied their voices seventy years ago because of a shameful criminal justice system that existed in Florida and throughout the Jim Crow South. We are a better state and a better country today because collectively we no longer tolerate gross perversions of justice like this. This Clemency process represents an opportunity to finally give voice to the Groveland Four, to tell them that after seventy years they are no longer powerless."

Senator Gary Farmer went next: "I was the sponsor of the resolution in the senate. I'm joined by Representative Bobby DuBose today. I've been asked to read into the record on behalf of family members who could not be here today a letter that has already been sent to all members of the Clemency Board. On behalf of our families, thank you very much for your attention to recognizing and correcting the injustices done to the Groveland Four. We greatly appreciate your public statements of support and the work you have done to place the issue on the Florida Board of Executive Clemency agenda. As nearly seventy years have passed since the four men were accused of crimes they didn't commit and received punishments they didn't deserve, we respectfully ask that you act quickly to pardon and exonerate the Groveland

Four. Posthumous pardon applications were previously filed on behalf of Mr. Charles Greenlee and Walter Irvin as they were the two members with active Florida convictions on their records. All of us, along with countless other advocates across Florida and the United States strongly urge you to grant these pardon applications and ask the FDLE to clear their names and give the Greenlee and Irvin families the justice they deserve.

We are also writing to ask that you give equal consideration to the cases of Ernest Thomas and Samuel Shepherd. While neither Mr. Thomas nor Mr. Shepherd technically have current Florida convictions, both are deserving of similar exonerations by the Clemency Board and FDLE. After being accused in 1949, Mr. Thomas was executed by a mob before he could enter the court system. Samuel Shepherd was wrongfully convicted by an all-white Lake County jury and sentenced to death. With the help of Thurgood Marshall, Mr. Shepherd appealed and the Supreme Court overturned his conviction and remanded the case for a new trial. But Sam Shepherd never made it to a new trial. Sheriff Willis McCall murdered him in cold blood before he could ever return to Lake County.

The rules of executive clemency provide broad pardon authority. As Rule 4 states, a full pardon forgives guilt for any Florida convictions. The Rules even allow pardons without a conviction. As stated in Rule 5, persons who had adjudication of guilt withheld and were not convicted may apply for a pardon if they otherwise meet the eligibility requirements of this rule. Justice for both Ernest Thomas and Samuel Shepherd would well be within the letter and spirit of those rules.

This week the Orlando Sentinel reported that family members of the Groveland Four accuser had written to the clemency board members in a last minute effort to block justice, stating:

Though we are saddened by their actions it does not appear they have encountered any of the overwhelming evidence of innocence. That evidence convinced the City of Groveland, Lake County, all five Lake County Constitutional officers, including the current sheriff, U.S. Senator Marco Rubio and the Florida legislature that Mr. Greenlee, Mr. Irvin, Mr. Shepherd, and Mr. Thomas were wronged and deserve vindication. It should convince you as well. You have the power in your hand to right the wrongs done to the Groveland Four and clear their names. We ask that you use that power now to end seventy years of injustice. On behalf of our families, please pardon and exonerate Charles Greenlee, Walter Irvin, Sam Shepherd, and Ernest Thomas. Thank you for your public service and consideration of our families' request for justice."

Next up, **two officials from Lake County**: Carey Baker, the property appraiser, representing all five constitutional officers; and Leslie Campione, Chairman of the Board of County Commissioners for Lake County, representing the entire commission. They pled for a pardon, citing the lack of due process in a case where the process for true justice was so egregiously flawed, so twisted, so perverted, and the actions of local law enforcement so terrible, that true justice could never prevail. The only real remedy, they said, was a full pardon for those accused.

Representative Geraldine Thompson spoke next: She recounted how when she served in the Florida Senate she was contacted by family members of the Groveland Four and asked to sponsor legislation to pardon them, which she did. There is a lot that is painful in our history, she said, and we are not responsible for what happened in 1949, but we are responsible for what happens on our watch and this is our watch. I'm asking you to take the final step to exonerate the Groveland Four and to finally show that Florida has leaders who listen who care and want to show that we value all people here in the great sunshine state.

What happened next can only be described as courtroom drama.

A black woman stepped up to the microphone and introduced herself as Beverly Robinson, first cousin to Samuel Shepherd and one of the family members who had asked Senator Thompson to sponsor a bill. She argued that the right word is exonerate, not pardon, because the attack never happened. Then she recounted how, as a professor teaching a course on cultural diversity in Florida some years back, she had asked her students to write an essay about the first time they encountered racism in their lives. She was shocked when one the essays gave a detailed account of what happened that night in Groveland. It was written by Norma Padgett's niece and in it she said the events never happened and that the family had been sworn to secrecy.

Then Beverly Robinson looked straight at Norma Padgett and declared: *You all are liars, Ms. Padgett.* She ended her speech by asking the Board for exoneration.

Wow, that was a hard act to follow and I was up next. After introducing myself, I said that I was the one who had submitted the applications for pardon. Then I continued:

"Four years ago, I was a student at the University of Florida and in my American History class we read *Devil in the Grove* by Gilbert King. I was twenty years old, focused on what my major was going to be and what I was going to do with my life, but I read that book and immediately felt like I had to do something about this. I started doing research and spoke to Carol Greenlee, Vivian Shepherd, Wade Greenlee, and every member of this family. I spoke to Gilbert King, I worked with Senator Farmer and Representative DuBose and for the last four years we've been working to make this happen because it's the right thing to do. Four years ago I created an online petition asking for exoneration of the Groveland Four and since that time we've had almost 10,000 signatures from five countries, all fifty states, and over a hundred cities in the state of Florida. There was even a fifth grader in Fort Lauderdale who started a letter writing campaign to our elected officials because this impacted him. I think we can see that this affected people seventy years ago, is still impacting people today and impacts our future and where we go from here. I appreciate your time and consideration."

I was the last person who spoke in favor of the pardon, which meant the next speaker was Norma Padgett, herself.

"I'm the victim of that night," she began, "and I tell you now that it's been on my mind for seventy years. I was seventeen years old and it's never left my mind. I'm begging y'all not to give the pardons because they did it. If you do, you're going to be just like them. You all just don't know what kind of horror I've been through for all these many years. I don't want them pardoned, no I do not. And you wouldn't either."

It was a powerful testimonial and she seemed to sincerely believe she was speaking the truth. She didn't come off as senile or confused in any way--but nothing she said had any basis in fact. The physician who had examined her all those years ago found no evidence of sexual assault; witnesses said she had not been assaulted, and let's have a reality check, Charles Greenlee was put in jail the minute he got off the bus in Groveland. Yet Norma held this story out as her truth.

Norma was followed by two of her sons and a daughter-in-law, who said they loved her and believed her and that she was not a liar.

As there were no more speakers, the Governor took the floor.

Governor Ron DeSantis: "In 2017, the FL Legislature passed a resolution as has been alluded to that said in part that the Groveland Four were victims of gross injustices and abhorrent treatment by the criminal justice system as a shameful chapter in this state's history and they asked the governor at the time for an expedited review of the case and with me as the governor now I take that under advisement. In the words of one of the leading Supreme Court Justices of his generation, Robert Jackson, this is one of the best examples of one of the worst menaces to American justice.

I believe in the principles of the Constitution, I believe in getting a fair shake. You'd like to think that in America no matter what passions or prejudices may be on the outside of a courtroom that when you get into the courtroom that it's the law applied to facts without passion or prejudice that will decide your fate. I don't think there's any way you can look at this case and think those ideals of justice were satisfied. Indeed they were perverted time and time again. And I think the way this was carried out was a miscarriage of justice and I am mindful of some of the statements from people in Lake County and I think it says a lot about them that they're willing to acknowledge that this was not right. At this time, the appropriate thing to do is to move to grant pardons--not just for Charles Greenlee and Walter Irvin, who have records, but all members of the Groveland Four."

It was so moved and seconded by the Committee members.

The Governor concluded: "Today we have taken action to pardon the Groveland Four and while this act cannot right the wrongs done to them many years ago, I hope that it will bring peace to their families and their communities.

Nikki Fried added: "I am so thankful for us bringing this up on the agenda today and I am asking for a proclamation exonerating all four."

Ashley Moody, the Attorney General, said: "I hope that the press will leave the victim and her family in peace."

The meeting was adjourned to thunderous clapping--and rejoicing!

Post-Pardon

 *"It always seems impossible until it's done."*

Nelson Mandela

IF I WAS HAVING TROUBLE BELIEVING THE PARDONS REALLY happened, all I had to do was read the headlines--this was national news!

Carol's reaction*: "It is a weight lifted, it is a cloud lifted. It's the dignity of being a Greenlee restored, it's the shame taken away, it's being let out of prison from a lie that has plagued our family for all these years. It's being relieved of not being able to say that you're a Greenlee. It's just so overwhelming. It's like waking up out of a nightmare, out of a terrible dream."*

Gilbert's reaction*: The pardons were remarkable, and the entire day was surreal. After years of incremental progress, suddenly everything came together in rapid speed. I was actually surprised that the Clemency Board moved to a vote. I did not expect that to happen on that day. I'm reminded of a great quote from Gloria Steinem. "Whenever one person* *stands up and says, 'Wait a minute, this is wrong,'' it helps other people do the same.'' That quote reminds me of Josh, and the role he played in correcting a decades-old injustice.*

Bobby DuBose's reaction: *When Governor DeSantis granted their pardons, it was an amazing feeling – finally, justice was served! My takeaway from the experience is that the process is <u>extremely</u> political and it takes the <u>right person</u> at the <u>right time</u> to make it happen. I feel fortunate and humbled to have undertaken this project – it was worth the fight.*

Ben Polsky's reaction: *I wasn't there in person and we didn't know until very end that Governor Desantis would pardon them in his first cabinet meeting. I watched the session and was very proud of our governor: He spoke of owning up to our state's history that these men didn't get a fair trial and I really respected the way he handled the last minute tensions between the Groveland men's families and the accuser and her family. I also learned it takes a team of dedicated people to organize but that if you do and the politics line up, you can actually make a difference. I feel so happy for the families of the Groveland boys. My classmates learned that if they jump in and get involved, their voices matter. I hope they feel empowered and take that sense of empowerment into other areas of their lives.*

Kalia Jones's reaction: *I have never been so happy! I felt like I could really make a difference, even at such a young age. This journey changed my life because I realized that doing the right thing and helping other people is the most rewarding thing someone can do. Not only does it make them happier but you also get to fill yourself with happiness. I want to help more people and be as involved as I possibly can so that I can create a ripple effect of happiness throughout the world.*

———

On June 23, 2019, Chris Hand and Lori Kifer Johnson won the 2019 "but for Leadership Florida" award for launching a campaign in 2018 to clear the names of the Groveland Four by raising awareness, educating influencers and forcing change. They initiated a full advocacy plan and leveraged their connections with Leadership Florida Cornerstone Class 36 classmates and their networks to educate the Florida State Board of Executive Clemency, seeking posthumous pardons.

Farewell, Petition

 *"In the end, it's all about perseverance."*

Dean Koontz

I VISITED OUR CHANGE.ORG PETITION ONE LAST TIME, THE same day the pardon was granted. We had 9,757 supporters who hailed from all fifty states, five countries, over a hundred cities in Florida and over three hundred cities in the U.S. Taking a trip down memory lane I reread my Petition updates which are shared below. Out of curiosity, I looked up the last person to sign the petition. Her name is Meredith Johnson and her comment was: "For Justice!"

What a perfect ending. Thank you, Meredith.

Exonerate The Groveland Four

MARCH 28, 2015 — Everyone, thank you so much for signing! 180 signatures is great

but we have a long way to go! Please continue to share the petition with your friends and family.

2,000 signatures!

SEPTEMBER 29, 2015 —Thank you so much to everyone for their support! A big thank you to Leonard Pitts Jr. for his amazing article. There is a bill in the Florida Senate that Senator Geraldine Thompson has proposed, seeking exoneration and an apology. The petition is more important now than ever!

5,000 signatures!

OCTOBER 16, 2015 —Thank you so much for the overwhelming support from across 45 states and several countries! There has been so much kindness and compassion for the victims and their families, as well as anger and outrage at this injustice. We have been so impressed with people's desire to reach out and help right this wrong. We need to keep the momentum going and keep the signatures coming to support Senator Geraldine Thompson's bill to exonerate the men. The next step is contacting Representative Larry Metz and asking him to sponsor Senator Thompson's bill.

Thank you everyone,

Josh Venkataraman and Carol Greenlee

NOVEMBER 9, 2015 —Our petition to exonerate The Groveland Four recently hit 6,000! Now we need to take it to the next level and we need your help. If you can, please take a minute and send a message to Florida Representative Larry Metz. You can cut and paste the message below. It's time our voices were heard!

Thank-you,

Josh and Carol

Dear Representative Metz:

Please consider co-sponsoring Senator Thompson's Bill to exonerate The Groveland Four. This terrible injustice still hangs over the people of Florida to this day. Exoneration, while symbolic, would give some peace to the families and to the Groveland community. After 66 years, exoneration is long overdue and it's also the right thing to do. Thank-you

We're almost there!

MARCH 9, 2016 —We are getting closer to this exoneration than we could have ever imagined! On February 16th, the city of Groveland issued a proclamation asking Governor Rick Scott to exonerate the Groveland Four. This upcoming Tues-

day, March 15th, Lake County will be issuing a similar proclamation. This is all thanks to every single person that signed
our petition, so thank you! But we're not quite there yet. If
you are so inclined, please send a letter to Governor Rick
Scott asking for exoneration. Once you've written the letter,
take a picture of it and post it to social media with the hashtag: #cleartheGrovelandFour

Thank you so much!

Send to:

Office of Governor Rick Scott

State of Florida

The Capitol

400 S. Monroe St.

Tallahassee, FL 32399-0001

DECEMBER 20, 2016 —Hi everyone. It's been a long fight
but we're not finished yet. We're still trying to get at least
10,000 signatures on the petition to increase awareness of the
case and our cause. We do have some updates though:

• Lionsgate is ramping up for production on "The Devil in the
Grove" film

• There is another production company working on a potential documentary focused on the petition and our fight for
exoneration

• We are working to have a bill proposed in the Florida House
and Senate for a legal exoneration of the Groveland Four

The two ways you can help are to share the petition with your
friends and family on social media and to contact your
Florida Senators and Representatives to ask them for their

support for exoneration of the Groveland Four in the 2017 session.

Thank you all for your continued support to right this wrong.

FEBRUARY 15, 2017 — Hi everyone, Thank you so much for your continued support. The newest update is that due to the success of the petition, Florida Senator Gary Farmer and Representative Bobby DuBose have filed a joint resolution asking the state of Florida to exonerate the Groveland Four. This is the closest we have ever been to righting this horrible injustice so we couldn't be more grateful for this bill. If you are so inclined to contact your state senators and representatives and tell them you support this bill, we believe that would be beneficial to the passing of the legislation.

We Have Work to Do!

MARCH 27, 2017 — Hi all, Thank you for your continued support. We are so close to achieving exoneration but now comes the hard part. We need your help. If everyone could call the office of these representatives and tell them that you'd like them to support Bill HCR 631 regarding the Groveland Four, it would make a world of difference!

Please spread the word!

APRIL 17, 2017 — Hi all, As a result of our hard work and passion, the Groveland Four will receive an apology and a pardon from Governor. Rick Scott and the state of Florida.

The Senate bill will pass sometime between 10AM and 12PM and the House bill will pass sometime between 1PM and 7PM with a potential press conference at Noon. Thank you all for your support.

APRIL 22, 2017 —Hi all, I apologize for all the updates but this was an exciting week.

The Florida House voted unanimously to clear the Groveland Four and formally apologize to their families for what was done so many years ago. The Senate will be passing the bill next week and Governor Rick Scott will be signing the bill and making it official. Thank you all for helping us continue the work of Thurgood Marshall.

DECEMBER 21, 2018 —Newly-elected incoming Governor Ron DeSantis has promised that a pardon for the Groveland Four will be a priority immediately when he begins his term. Please continue to push and share the petition so that we can show our legislators that 10,000+ support this pardon!

Victory!

JANUARY 11, 2019 —Thank you to everyone for signing and joining this cause. Today Governor DeSantis and the Florida Cabinet voted to pardon all four of the Groveland Four. We couldn't have done this without you. Thank you, sincerely.

Post-Script

 *Every accomplishment starts with the decision to try.*

John F. Kennedy

How do you measure success? For Carol, it was exoneration or bust, but there were many successes along the way. Her ultimate goal was to clear her father's name, to make some good come out of this horrible event--and didn't she achieve just that? One could argue that Gilbert's book cleared her father's name. One could argue that the 10,000 people signing a petition demanding justice for her father and the other men was a form of justice. One could argue that receiving public apologies from Groveland and Lake County was a form of justice and an acknowledgment that her father was innocent. One could argue that the multitude of press clamoring for justice and bringing this story to light was a measure of her success. One could argue that the Florida legislature publicly acknowledging the innocence of the four men and apologizing to the families was justice. Although the pardon was finally granted, if it hadn't been, wouldn't the project have been a success anyway?

I hope this story provides some perspective on how much time it takes to get results (who can say?) and who might help you (anyone you can get) and how you will recognize you've reached a tipping point where success is inevitable (you may not know).

Think about all the obstacles we faced: no signers for the petition, Senator Thompson's proposed legislation failing to draw a House sponsor twice; the governor refusing to take action after the meeting with the Lake County officials and after the joint resolution from the legislature; the problem with the language of exoneration vs. pardon; UF law school having a different vision for the forum; our assumption that an application for a pardon had already been filed, then having to file an application for a pardon seventy years after the fact--just to name a few. We could have given up so many times. But we didn't.

It's great to have a plan, but ours was very basic--start a petition and get people to sign it. Even with a more elaborate plan we would have had to change course so many times we would have thrown it out the window. There's a Zen saying: All you need, you already have. If you embrace that philosophy, you realize you can find the resources and people to help you.

How's this for a crazy plan: start a petition on Change.org; convince a nationally syndicated Pulitzer Prize winning journalist to write a column about it; ask Florida Trend Magazine to write a feature article; convince Gilbert King and the UF law school to host a panel about the Groveland Four and convince Sam Harris to come make a public apology to the families; encourage Senator Thompson to refile her bill; then ask Groveland and Lake County officials to issue public apologies and also convince them to take up the cause with the Governor; convince Margaret Grostefon to speak with Gary Farmer whom she met by chance and solicit his help; convince

Gary Farmer to sponsor a bill and ask if he happens to have a friend in the House he can approach to sponsor a companion bill; convince every Florida Representative to co-sponsor the bill and then convince the entire Florida Legislature to pass the joint resolution apologizing to the families and urging the governor to exonerate them; write an application for pardons, convince Gary Farmer to enlist Chris Hand to lobby for pardons and exert public pressure on officials; convince a public relations firm to take up the cause pro bono to keep the story in the news; and, finally, convince the new administration (also majority Republican like the last administration) to hold a clemency hearing within two weeks of taking office and grant pardons for all four men (which the last administration said couldn't be done) Sounds like a plan to me! I'm game, are you?

Whatever your cause, be flexible, be passionate, and above all, be persistent and you will accomplish great things. I can't wait to hear about them!

Timeline

1949--July 16th The Groveland Four are falsely accused of rape by Norma Padgett and three of them are subsequently convicted.

1951--November Thurgood Marshall succeeds in having the convictions overturned by the U.S. Supreme Court. Sheriff McCall shoots Walter Irvin and Sam Shepherd while transporting them, killing Shepherd and grievously injuring Irvin.

2012--March *Devil in the Grove: Thurgood Marshall, the Groveland Boys, and the Dawn of a New America* is published.

2013 Gilbert King wins a Pulitzer Prize.

2014--Fall I read the book as a junior in an American History class at University of Florida.

2015-- I see the sign for Groveland on the highway.

2015--March Carol and I start the petition.

2015--Sept. 26th Leonard Pitts, Jr. writes first article about Groveland/Josh/Carol.

2015---Oct. 9th First article in Independent Florida Alligator. Petition has 3,000 signatures. I am a senior at University of Florida.

2015--December Florida Trend Magazine publishes an article about the case.

2015/16 Senator Geraldine Thompson, D-Orlando, files a proposed resolution (SCR 136) for consideration during the 2016 legislative session, her second attempt.

2015--Thanksgiving I meet Henrietta Irvin in Miami.

2015--December I meet with Gilbert in New York and come up with panel event.

2016--February 18 Panel discussion on the Groveland Four case at UF Levin College of Law. I meet Carol in person for the first time after working together long-distance for a year.

2016--February 16th Groveland and Lake County officials offer public apologies to the families and start lobbying state lawmakers to do the same.

2016--May Lake County officials meet with Governor Rick Scott's staff.

2016--May 23 Time interview with Gilbert.

2016--July Ben Polsky writes his children's book.

2016--November Gary Farmer is elected and I talk to him a few days later.

2016--December 24th Senator Gary Farmer plans to file a bill.

2017--March 6th Senator Farmer introduces Senate Resolution 920 in front of the criminal justice committee asking the at Governor exonerate the men and pardon Greenlee and Irvin. Representative Bobby Dubose files Resolution 631 with the House.

2017-March 20th Representative Bobby Dubose presents "Through Our Eyes--Remembering the Groveland Four".

2017--April 18th The Florida House of Representatives passes a resolution (HCR 631) exonerating the four men and apologizing to their families for the racial injustice of the case. The Senate passes a similar resolution. Lawmakers also call on Florida Governor Scott to officially pardon the men. The bill "extends a heartfelt apology" and acknowledges that the men "were the victims of gross injustices and that their abhorrent treatment by the criminal justice system is a shameful chapter in this state's history."

2017--May 2nd Leonard Pitts Jr. writes a second column saying the apology falls short of being justice.

2017--summer I file the application for pardons.

2019--January 4th I receive an email from clemency board.

2019--January 10th The Orlando Sentinel apologizes.

2019--January 11th The Florida Board of Executive Clemency votes to pardon the Groveland Four. I close out the petition on Change.org.

2020--February 21st The Groveland Four Memorial, commissioned by the Lake County Commission, is unveiled in front of the Old Lake County Courthouse. The four-foot tall granite and bronze monument is dedicated by Governor DeSantis and other elected officials in front of a crowd that includes family members of the Groveland Four. Both Carol Greenlee and Gilbert King are there to speak.

Dear reader,

We hope you enjoyed reading *Accidental Activist*. Please take a moment to leave a review, even if it's a short one. Your opinion is important to us.

Discover more books by Barbara Venkataraman at https://www.nextchapter.pub/authors/barbara-venkataraman

Want to know when one of our books is free or discounted? Join the newsletter at http://eepurl.com/bqqB3H

Best regards,

Barbara Venkataraman and the Next Chapter Team

About The Authors

Award-winning author Barbara Venkataraman is an attorney in South Florida where she draws inspiration for her books from the daily headlines. She loves connecting with readers through her books and finds a particular kind of joy in a well-turned phrase. In addition to writing fiction, she co-authored *Accidental Activist: Justice for the Groveland Four* with her son Josh Venkataraman about his successful four-year quest to obtain posthumous pardons for The Groveland Four.

Josh Venkataraman is the award-winning co-author of *Accidental Activist: Justice for the Groveland Four* and a recipient of the ViacomCBS Social Impact Award for his work on racial and social justice issues.

ENDNOTES

CHAPTER 3: PASSION PROJECT

1. G.King, *Devil in the Grove: Thurgood Marshall, the Groveland Boys, and the Dawn of a New America* (HarperCollins Publishers, 2013).

CHAPTER 4: POSTING A PETITION

1. Wkipedia.org, "Change.org", https://en.wikipedia.org/wiki/Change.org.

2. D. Cohea, "Justice in the Grove," Medium.com, December 20, 2105, https://medium.com/mountdora-topics/justice-in-the-grove-74fc1e58a627.

CHAPTER 5: PUBLICITY PLEASE

1. L. Pitts Jr., "Injustice That Has Never Been Corrected," *The Miami Herald*, September 27, 2015, 5B.

2. Wkipedia.org, "Leonard Pitts", https://en.wikipedia.org/wiki/Leonard_Pitts.

3. M. Vassolo, "UF Student Fights For Justice for Accused Rapists," *The Independent Florida Alligator*, October 9, 2015, Vol. 110, Issue 34.

4. C. Hayes, "UF Student's Petition Asks for Groveland Four to be Cleared of Crimes," *OrlandoSentinel.com*, October19, 2015, https://www.orlandosentinel.com/news/lake/os-groveland-four-uf-student-petition-apology-20151019-story.html.

5. L. Ritchie, "Petition on Groveland Four Revives Painful Past," *Orlando Sentinel*, October 23, 2015, https://www.

orlandosentinel.com/news/lake/os-lk-lauren-ritchie-groveland-four-petition-20151023-column.html.

6. A. Levy, "Florida Originals: A Stain on Florida's History," *Florida Trend, The Magazine of Florida*, December 2015, page 10.

CHAPTER 6: PUBLIC PARTICIPATION

1. K. Newberg, "The Groveland Four: A Meeting a Levin College of Law," *Alligator.org*, February 18, 2016, https://www.alligator.org/news/local/article_4063ae96-d6c2-11e5-b06d-bb9b6cb08225.html.

CHAPTER 7: BEN POLSKY

1. N. Polsky & B. Polsky, *Re-Righting History: The Groveland Boys* (CreateSpace Independent Publishing Platform, September 1, 2016).

CHAPTER 8: POLITICIANS

1. R. Brown, "Groveland Four Proclamation Sparks Threats," *DailyCommercial.com*, February 12, 2016, https://www.dailycommercial.com/article/20160212/News/302129994.

2. L. Stanford, "Advocates for Groveland Four Say Governor's Staff Was Doubtful About Pardon," *DailyCommercial.com*, May 21, 2016, https://www.dailycommercial.com/article/20160521/news/305219993?template=ampart.

CHAPTER 9: MORE PUBLICITY

1. M. Stone, "Behind the Search for an Apology in the Infamous 1949 'Groveland Boys' Case," Time.com, May 23, 2016, https://time.com/4343491/groveland-boys-gilbert-king/.

CHAPTER 11: MORE POLITICIANS

1. L. Ritchie, "County Commission Oks Groveland Four Resolution," *Daily Commercial*, March 1, 2016, https://www. dailycommercial.com/news/article_58837b89-fd60-5594-95be-c64e0c038e0d.html.

CHAPTER 13: PROMISES KEPT

1. G. Corsair, *The Groveland Four: The Sad Saga of a Legal Lynching* (AuthorHouse March 8, 2004).

2. Wkipedia.org, "The Dozier School for Boys," https://en. wikipedia.org/wiki/Florida_School_for_Boys.

CHAPTER 14: POST-RESOLUTION

1. G. Rohrer, "The State of Florida Was Wrong," *SunSentinel.com*, April 19, 2017.

2. B. Larabee, "Senate Tries to Bring Peace with Groveland Four Apology," *MiamiHerald.com*, April 27, 2017, https://www. miamiherald.com/news/politics-government/state-politics/ article147279614.html.

3. L. Pitts Jr., "Apology After 70 Years Falls Short of Being Justice," *The Miami Herald*, May 3, 2017, 13A.

4. S. Powers, "Rick Scott's office: Governor is Aware of Groveland Four Case, reviewing all options." November 29, 2017, *FloridaPolitics.com*, https://floridapolitics.com/archives/ 250635-rick-scotts-office-governor-aware-groveland-four-case-reviewing-options.

CHAPTER 15: THE PRESS PRESSES ON

1. S. Powers, "Where are the Groveland Four Pardons?" *FloridaPolitics.com*, November 20, 2017, https://floridapolitics.com/ archives/249971-groveland-four-pardons-story-continues-silence

2. S. Powers, "Rick Scott's office: Governor is Aware of Groveland Four Case, reviewing all options." November 29, 2017, *FloridaPolitics.com*, https://floridapolitics.com/archives/250635-rick-scotts-office-governor-aware-groveland-four-case-reviewing-options.

3. B. Graham & C. Hand, *America, the Owner's Manual: You Can Fight City Hall-and Win*, (CQ Press; New edition, August 16, 2016).

4. L. Ritchie, "Demand Justice for the Groveland Four, Black Men Framed and Killed by Racist Sheriff," *Orlando.Sentinel.com*, September 7, 2018, https://www.orlandosentinel.com/news/lake/os-lauren-ritchie-groveland-four-pardon-20180907-story.html

5. S. Powers, "Democrats for Cabinet Calling for Groveland Four Pardons, Republicans Mum," *FloridaPolirics.*com, September 10, 2018, https://floridapolitics.com/archives/274106-democrats-for-cabinet-calling-for-groveland-four-pardons-republicans-mum.

6. Editorial Board, Tallahassee Democrat, "The Clemency Board Must Act Now and Pardon the Groveland Four," *Tallahassee.com*, December 2, 2018, https://www.tallahassee.com/story/news/2018/12/01/clemency-board-must-act-now-and-pardon-groveland-four/2160437002/.

7. S. Powers, "No pardons in Line for Groveland Four as Rick Scott, Clemency Board Postpone Meeting," *FloridaPolitics.com*, December 3, 2018, https://floridapolitics.com/archives/282299-no-pardons-in-line-for-groveland-four-as-rick-scott-clemency-board-postpone-meeting.

CHAPTER 16: POPULAR AT LAST

1. L. Mower, "They Were Wrongly Accused of Raping a Woman. Will Florida's Groveland Four Be Pardoned?" *Miami-*

Herald.com, December 17, 2018, https://www.miamiherald.com/latest-news/article223195945.html.

2. S. Powers, "Jimmy Patronis Seeking Groveland Four Pardons," *FloridaPolitics.com*, December 19, 2018, https://floridapolitics.com/archives/283779-jimmy-patronis-seeking-groveland-four-pardons.

3. S. Powers, "Marco Rubio Calls for Justice for Groveland Four," *OrlandoWeekly.com*, December 19, 2018, https://floridapolitics.com/archives/283756-marco-rubio-calls-for-justice-for-groveland-four.

4. J. Turner, "Ron DeSantis Plans to make Pardons for Groveland Four a Priority," *OrlandoWeekly.com*, December 21, 2018, https://www.orlandoweekly.com/Blogs/archives/2018/12/21/ron-desantis-plans-to-make-pardons-for-groveland-four-a-priority.

CHAPTER 17: TO PARDON OR NOT TO PARDON

1. Orlando Sentinel Editorial Board, "To the Community and the Families of the Groveland Four: We're Sorry," *Orlando Sentinel*, January 19, 2019, https://www.orlandosentinel.com/opinion/editorials/os-op-orlando-sentinel-apologizes-groveland-four-20190109-story.html.

2. Clemency hearing: https://thefloridachannel.org/videos/1-11-19-executive-clemency-board-meeting/

CHAPTER 18: POST-PARDON

1. LeadershipFlorida.org, "Announcing 2019 "but for Leadership Florida" Award," June 28, 2019, https://www.leadershipflorida.org/news/announcing-2019-but-for-leadership-florida-award-winners.

Accidental Activist
ISBN: 978-4-86752-322-3

Published by
Next Chapter
1-60-20 Minami-Otsuka
170-0005 Toshima-Ku, Tokyo
+818035793528

15th October 2021